THE DIRECTOR'S COMPANION

THE DIRECTOR'S COMPANION

MEL SHAPIRO

University of California, Los Angeles

THOMSON
WADSWORTH

Australia • Canada • Mexico • Singapore • Spain • United Kingdom • United States

Publisher	Earl McPeek
Acquisitions Editor	Barbara J. C. Rosenberg
Product Manager	Pat Murphree
Developmental Editor	Steve Stembridge
Project Editor	Sandy Walton
Art Director	Candice Johnson Clifford
Production Manager	Linda McMillan

Cover and part opener photography by Dan Bryant. Appearing courtesy of their owners are Madonna, Joshua, Shelby, Nicholas, Emily, and Scout.

ISBN: 0-15-503103-1
Library of Congress Catalog Card Number: 97-73576

Wadsworth Group/Thomson Learning
10 Davis Drive
Belmont CA 94002-3098
USA

For information about our products, contact us:
Thomson Learning Academic Resource Center
1-800-423-0563
http://www.wadsworth.com

For permission to use material from this text, contact us by
Web: http://www.thomsonrights.com
Fax: 1-800-730-2215
Phone: 1-800-730-2214

Copyright/acknowledgment: Pages 153–156 storyboard drawings for *The House of Blue Leaves,* by Fred Tatasciore.

Printed in the United States of America
25 24 23 22

To Josh and Ben

Acknowledgements

I want to thank Rich Rose for collaborating with me on the chapter on groundplans and supplying his drawings; Fred Tatasciore for his illustrations; Karl Eigsti for his groundplan to *The House of Blue Leaves* and his sketches for *Long Day's Journey into Night* and *Sergeant Musgrave's Dance;* Leon Katz for his piece on dramaturgy; John Guare for the use of sections of *The House of Blue Leaves;* Zelda Fichandler; John Wray for his notes on his "How I Spent My ___Vacation" exercise; Nancy Keystone for saving those old class notes; Maggie Rowe and Christopher Fairbanks, Rick Roemer, Danny Kaufman, Consuello Diaz, Stephen Burdman, Rob Lyons, Ruben Polendo, and Vicky Smith for participating in the "Symposium on Directing," and finally, a note of gratitude to my teacher Larry Carra and my great mentor Ted Hoffman.

PREFACE

People often say to me, "You teach directing! I didn't know it could be taught." They look at me like I'm a junk bond salesman or the perpetrator of a national hoax. My response to them is, "Directing is like all other arts . . . or if that word is too pretentious, it's like all other crafts: It's self-taught. What I do is help people teach themselves." This usually satisfies the interrogator, but he or she will then persist with, "How do you teach them to teach themselves? Do you tell them stories about your own experiences and that of others?" I tell them absolutely not. I never tell any anecdotes about show business or theatre lore as I know it. Early in my teaching career I started telling a story about a show I'd done, and a young woman raised her hand and said, "I don't want to hear your anecdotes. I don't want to live vicariously through your experiences. I want to have my own!" Since then I've told no anecdotes. Except one. Maybe two. But the one I always tell has a lot to do with whether or not directing can be taught, and I'm going to tell it now.

I'd been in the army, got involved in the English-speaking theatre in Japan, and when I was discharged enrolled as a student in the drama department at the Carnegie Institute of Technology in Pittsburgh, Pennsylvania. My directing teacher there was a man named Larry Carra, who had written a book with Alexander Dean called the *Fundamentals of Play Directing*. I adored Larry but hated his book with a passion. The reasons were many. We had to memorize vast sections of it and were subjected to "spot quizzes" at a moment's notice. What the book deemed to be verities of stagecraft I found questionable. And because the book was treated like our catechism, dogmatic and inflexible, I found myself rebelling at it every chance I could. Yet, Larry himself was an extremely original and insightful teacher who, I must confess, was always slyly amused by my rebellion of the sacred text. Years later I came to realize that although I may have rebelled and struggled against "the Fundies," as we called Larry's approach, at least I learned them. But by the time I graduated, I felt that I had learned nothing and that whatever was positive in my work was due to my own brilliance.

When I began to work professionally, a very odd thing happened. Whenever I felt doubt or hesitation in a rehearsal, I would hear Larry's voice in my ear telling me what to do. "Move her to the right to balance the stage," "The composition is out of focus. She should move more to the center of the stage!" I literally felt that I was possessed by some kind of directorial dybbuk in Larry's voice, guiding me through the rough moments. But like St. Joan, the voices that I once heard no longer spoke to me. I was on my own, and Larry Carra became a distant memory.

When we did *Two Gentlemen of Verona* as a musical in Central Park in New York it was a great success and was moved to Broadway. Between the park and Broadway we set about fixing the areas that we knew were weak, such as the first twenty minutes of the show. By the time we were in previews at the St. James theatre, the first twenty minutes that didn't work were now forty minutes that didn't work. Talk about improvements! The audience kept walking out. One matinee six hundred people left at the intermission. Joe Papp, the producer, tried to lock up John Guare, Galt MacDermot, and myself in a hotel room until we solved the problem.

On the morning of the very last preview before opening night, about 5 A.M., I heard a knock on the door. It was John Guare, who had written the lyrics and coauthored the libretto. We knew that it was our last few hours to come to a solution. We had tried everything. We thought that the first part of the musical, which takes place in Verona, should be about friendship (there was a song about that), about leaving home (there was a song about that, too), about wooing (a song, of course), about wanting to invent a new life (a duet, naturally), and so forth.

We sat in silence all morning, wondering what had happened to the lovely little hit we had in Central Park, and with just a few hours to go before a noon rehearsal, Guare said to me, "What would Larry Carra say?" I thought that Guare had lost his mind right there in my kitchen. "John, why don't we run down to Bleecker Street and have some tea leaves read! What's Larry Carra got to do with any of this? You never even met the man." Guare said, "You told me once you used to hear him in your ear, telling you what to do. He was your teacher, what would he say?" I thought: This is the way all flops go — one of the partners cracks up. But in a few minutes I was able to say, "I think Larry would have said. . ." and I recalled his Boston accent very clearly, "What's the basic situation?" Guare said, "What's that?" I told him that in our case it would mean: "What, in the simplest terms, reduced to its essence, is the Verona sequence about?" We looked at each other and at the same time said, "It's about Julia falling in love!" The sequence had nothing to do with all the stuff we added. It was very simply about this young girl who falls in love. We ran to the theatre, cut two songs, rearranged the action, and rescued a song that had long been cut and that the composer, Galt MacDermot, had to play on the electric piano that night because there was no orchestration for it.

The show got a standing ovation. The next morning David Merrick bumped into us on Shubert Alley and said, "What did you boys do last night? It's the first time I ever heard word of mouth on a show go from disastrous to great. The news on the street is you're going to have a hit tonight."

Can directing be taught? Argue any way you like.

Can it be learned? Yes. And as you can see, usually the hard way.

CONTENTS

INTRODUCTON

This book does not intend to supplant other directing books that stress mechanics, theory, style, or concepts of directing. This book is about the practicalities of directing, born of many years' experience, and as such, it can be a companion to any text or any teacher's methodology.

This book is a thinly veiled autobiography posing as a textbook. I believe that much of art is autobiographical and that directing is as personal an act as writing or acting. Directing is an inner search into one's self for intuition, imagination, and guidance. There's a light that goes on, a voice that you hear or just a feeling about something that helps you know what it is you have to know at the moment you have to know it. I don't mean to make any of this mystical or to suggest that directing is an act of divination. Directing is a great deal of craft, technique, and experience, not to mention a great deal of paying one's dues. But you are the instrument through which the music plays. Are we magicians, conjuring dead authors, permitting them to speak through us? I don't think so, necessarily. But directing does often seem like an act of ventriloquism as the play is speaking through us.

As directors we live the life of the play so intensely that we graft our experiences and imagination onto it in the same way that it does onto us. Like an old married couple who finish each other's sentences and laugh at their own jokes, play and director similarly become one.

There is a misconception that has always bothered me, and that is the notion that directing is basically a very cerebral exercise and should be attempted only by graduate or postgraduate students. The theory here is that a director needs to know acting, design, art, architecture, music, history, philosophy, religion, literature, foreign languages, and all the sciences as well as having lived a rich, complex, and fascinating life before directing. Many universities have thrown out undergraduate directing programs for that reason. Paradoxically, however, it has been my long experience that although grad students are often very talented and passionately committed, some of the best work is often done by the undergraduates who are freer, less hung up on proving their intellectuality, and have nothing going for them but lots of ideas and imagination. What both groups lack is a trust in their own instincts. Getting students to trust their instincts is often what teaching any subject in the arts is all about. Yes, there are techniques and skills and practical experience, but that doesn't mean that while they're being acquired the student must erase himself.

If I tell a student that I'm interested in seeing what she has lived through, I'm greeted with astonishment. "Me, interesting? You mean I can put myself in the work? I count?"

I was fortunate enough to have the opportunities to direct before I had any formal training. By the time I got into technique classes, I had a frame of reference for them. Students today spend a great deal of time either theorizing about directing in seminars or are given too much foundation in technical matters before they've had any hands-on directing experience at all. It reminds me of singers who sing without any connection to what they are singing: They are intent on technically hitting the notes. It's an empty skill.

Lately, I've come to the conclusion that directing has to begin with:

- The courage to explore not only with the mind, but also with the emotional history that one has lived through.
- Plunging right in with exercises and extended theatre pieces, even before there's any talk of technique or a formal foundation. A frame of reference should be built by experiencing the power of putting one's ideas and feelings on the stage in front of one's peers.

I bring all this up to explain my particular approach to the subject. Now, we have to ask certain questions about the subject itself.

What is a director?

What does a director do?

How is it done?

This book is divided in five parts, exploring answers to those three questions. Part 1 is "The Director as Storyteller." This is the heart of the matter. The director's first and foremost job is to tell the story of the play. And because a storytelling ability is so important for the director to cultivate, I find it necessary to ask the student to begin with his or her own story. We do stage pieces based on autobiographical incidents. We begin to reignite our memory and use it to dramatic effect. Of course, we embellish it; we add theatrical spice to what's happened to us. We end up by bending time, heightening the details themselves, finding physical metaphors for inner feelings.

We see that the glue that holds a story together is dramatic tension. Now we go from our autobiography to dramatic tension and begin to add visualization. We begin to create images and pictures that help tell our story.

The way that most teaching and learning take place is through the critique. Critiquing is essentially about thinking. It's about how we solve a problem; and directing is about solving problems. Of course, you have to be able to locate a problem before you can begin to solve it. Until the student has learned to clearly, specifically, and constructively critique the work of others and take criticism himself, he will never be able to discern what works from what doesn't.

Part 2 is "The Director as Interpreter." If we were looking for a director and needed to state the job description, we would see that she would have to qualify on at least two counts: "Must be able to tell a story and interpret it as well." This section is one that I wish I had had in a book when I was studying, which is why I put it in now. I knew about play structure—somewhat—from writing and directing and taking drama history courses, but I never had it all put together for me in the same room. That room didn't exist until I was in rehearsal halls during professional situations, where I flew by the seat of my pants. By then, it was necessity that put it all together for me.

This section asks the director to explore:

What one's gut reaction to the material is.

What is the play about.

How the director makes what it's about happen onstage.

How the play has been built structurally.

Part 2 also deals with language. I promised myself I wasn't going to use this book as a forum to complain and rant. And the one thing I hated when I was young was listening to older people extol the "good old days of theatre"! But! I keep seeing productions where actors can't speak and directors don't seem to know it. Or if they know it, they don't care because they're so wrapped up in their concept and whatever agenda is in their head. The chapter on language attempts to address how to work with actors on building their characters through the words the author has chosen for them to speak. Naturally, the director must learn to become aware of language as well (if not more so).

Part 3 adds another element to the director's job description: "Must collaborate." "The Director as Collaborator" deals with the preparations that a director makes and how those preparations affect relationships with designers, playwrights, producers, and dramaturgs. Theatre, as we've heard over and over, is a collaborative art, which is part of its great joy and its great frustration. Collaboration ends up being a transaction between artists in which inspiration hopefully occurs and in which disagreements can be negotiated. The bottom line is always mutual respect for each other's work. This is especially true in the actor/director relationship, which is the most intense collaboration because it's about the human aspect of what's going to be put on the stage in front of an audience.

When I ask students what they would like to see in a book on directing, the first thing they say is, "How to work with actors." It helps if you have studied acting or have acted because you need to understand the nature of the process, which is different for each actor but also in many ways the same. The chapter on the actor/director collaboration gives various techniques and methods for working with actors and for sharing the development of the performances. It goes without saying that it helps the relationship if you like actors and are not intimidated by them.

Part 4 is "The Director as Stager." For me, getting down to staging the play is the best part of the work. Groundplans and blocking are discussed in this section, as well as composition and picturization. What's important here is that the student begin to be cognizant of these as tools of directing and to investigate them further through practical experience. The amount of didacticism on what makes a picture or what is a "pleasing" composition is daunting. One director's book suggests quite rightly that "picturization is an aspect of blocking that intensifies the storytelling values." But the author goes on to give examples such as:

"A dead body tends to be horizontal." Yes, it's horizontal if it's lying down. But what if it's standing in the closet or sitting at the dinner table?

"A person kneeling before a person standing is connotative of begging." Why begging? It is connotative of being subjugated, of confessing, or of fixing the hem on the trousers of the person standing.

The author continues with the list of examples, which are out of nineteenth-century melodrama or an acting style of another period.

Another author in his chapter on picturization says "the following is a table showing mood values of areas in terms of tonal qualities and suggested scenes":

Tonal Qualities in Each Area	Scenes Suggested
1. Down-center: hard, intense, harsh, strong, climactic, great formality	Quarrels, fights, crises, climaxes
2. Up-center: regal, aloof, noble, superiority, stability	Formal and romanticized love scenes, scenes of domination and judiciary nature, royalty
3. Down-right: warm, informal, tender	Intimate love scenes, informal calls, confessions, gossip, long narratives

These formalized rules of art have always annoyed me. The minute that I heard that fights should be down-center, I put one up-right. When I heard that down-right was warm and the place for an intimate love scene, I put it up-left where it's supposed to be isolated and cold, unfit for anything but the ghost of Hamlet's father. You can't deal in rules like these because everything depends on what else is going on on the stage and on what the story is. Otherwise you're staging clichés that the audience has seen millions of times.

For me the key to blocking is in how you stage the changing action in a scene. This is demonstrated by a section of John Guare's *The House of Blue Leaves*, which has been storyboarded to show how action and blocking go together.

Next we come to counterpoint.

I used to attend Saturday matinees of Broadway shows as I grew up and by the time I was a teenager fancied myself quite a connoisseur of the theatre. But after I saw the work of Tyrone Guthrie, I was forced to admit that I knew nothing. Guthrie would have a huge ensemble scene with a hundred people on the stage, when suddenly someone would appear on a level stage left. This person would give a speech, and when it was over, the audience would look down and see to its astonishment that those hundred people had vanished. Everyone would mutter, "How did he do that?" How did this wizard shift focus so suddenly that we didn't notice all those people leaving?" But more interestingly, Guthrie always had at least two or three scenes going onstage at the same time. You could be watching a scene where the dialogue was being spoken, but behind it, for instance, another scene was kept alive through movement and stage action, which never detracted from the scene with dialogue; if anything, it enhanced the dialogue. I would see the show a second and third time, just to watch how Guthrie manipulated the movement of each scene so that the eyes of the audience always knew where to focus and when to change that focus on to something else. I began noticing that this is something that films do all the time. Somewhere along the way I heard that this is called *counterpoint.* Not having the reader in the classroom or a video to demonstrate the technique, I have tried, without the narrative gifts of Marcel Proust, to describe it. But I hope that the films I've suggested will be rented by the reader to get a real feel for the topic.

Concept has become a big word in the theatre today. "What's your concept going to be?" I always think this question treats theatre like fashion design: "Are we going to have long skirts this year, or short ones? What's the concept this season?" Directors, of course, have concepts. They always have and always will, which makes them directors. They see how something should be put onstage. But although I admire and appreciate idiosyncratic and self-serving concepts for their own theatricality (having foisted one or two onto the world myself), I prefer a concept that reveals the play more than it does the director. In this section of part 4 two diaries (fictional) by student directors express their concepts and how they attempted to execute them in production.

Part 5 is a seminar with several graduate directing students. They were asked two questions. First, "What do you think ought to be in a book about directing for today's students?" Second, "What are your questions about directing?"

Each chapter is summarized in either a "Frequently Asked Questions" section or a "Checklist."

Do I think that students have changed in the course of almost three decades of teaching? Their passion for the work and yearning to be part of the theatre still move me. That's always been the same. I used to think that students had to learn everything that I knew in the first week of class. Now I know a little better: I don't know that much, therefore, they can take a little longer to learn it. Students have to make knowledge their own, in their own time, in their own way. This book hopefully shows that process with that freedom.

PART ONE

THE DIRECTOR
AS STORYTELLER

Exploring one's biography and responding instinctively.

Dramatic tension as the glue that binds narrative together.

The nature and importance of critiquing.

Using biography as extended theatrical projects.

Visual awareness and metaphor.

CHAPTER ONE

INSTINCTS AND STORYTELLING

Sometimes you can look at a painting and become so entranced by it that you find yourself entering it. It's as though you have magically stepped inside it and have become part of its world. A part of you is objective enough to know that you really haven't, but a large part of your imagination has been ignited enough for you to feel you are in there, sharing its mystery and understanding all the elements of the story that it's trying to tell.

There are dreams in which we participate subjectively and dreams in which we watch ourselves and others, almost as bystanders. And there are dreams in which we know that we are dreaming but still can't let go of the events that are being unraveled before us.

If you look around at the audience in a movie theatre during a very compelling film, you will see people who seem to have left their seats and entered the screen. They are riding with the story, running when the hero runs, shooting the villains when the heroine is in jeopardy, crying when something sad has happened, screaming when scary events rush at them. It's possible to feel this way with a good novel. You enter it so completely that you don't want it to end.

When a director reads a play for the first time, he or she always hopes that a similar kind of immersion, an experience of complete involvement, will happen. The director wants to be so engrossed in the story, so satisfied by it, that he will be able to share the excitement of this intense experience with the audience.

The obvious questions at this point are:

What if the director isn't that involved with the story but has to do the play anyway? Shouldn't he or she have enough technique to bring the audience into it as fully as possible?

Isn't a director always objective and always analytical? A director has to be involved in the play's structure and can't afford to get lost or overinvolved by the play's story.

The problem with this line of reasoning is that it assumes that the director's technique and craft skills are far more important than his or her instincts or intuition, that objective analysis is more important than emotional response. Of course, the argument against instinct and intuition is: "These are things that cannot be taught. Technical expertise and the mechanics of stagecraft can be taught and acquired." Furthermore, "You either have good instincts, or you don't, and if you don't, you shouldn't bother to direct."

The problem is: Who knows if you have good instincts or the kind of intuition that makes for an interesting director if you are never given the opportunity to find out? I know from my own experience: I began directing before I had a lesson. Years later when I acquired technique and style I looked back at photographs of those early shows and was stunned to see that actors were somehow in the right positions, the mood and atmosphere of the scenes seemed to be right, and actors weren't standing in front of each other or bumping into the furniture. Paradoxically, years later, when I supposedly should have known better, whenever I got into trouble on a show it was because of one simple reason: I had strayed from my instincts. I had very definite feelings about certain things in the beginning of rehearsal and let them go. I made things complicated, compromised, did things for the wrong reasons, lost sight of what the real issues were, and ended up with a mess. At times like that, when all seems lost and you are in practically the last preview, someone will say something to you about the show, and you will hear yourself say, "Of course! I knew that on the first day of rehearsal! Why didn't I do it? Why didn't I listen to what I knew? Why didn't I trust my instincts?"

The most important qualities that a director has are instinct and intuition. You can stage with the wizardry of Tyrone Guthrie or the razzle-dazzle of Tommy Tune. Your technical grasp of movement, rhythm, timing, dynamics, and invention can be at the highest level. But everything you do is informed by your feelings, your intuition, your instincts about the material. And these feelings will tell you what the material means and how it should be presented. In other words, your intuitive response to the story and to how it's being told moment to moment is the strongest thing that you have as a director.

Story and Intuition

This will be the beginning of our work. And to a larger extent, it will be the basis of all the work we will do as directors.

The stories that we will start with will be our own: aspects, memories, incidents, and events from our own lives. Great tales of fiction by famous authors will be dealt with later. Right now, we are going to put autobiographical pieces onto the stage. And because we haven't discussed any of the fundamentals of directing yet, you are going to have to fly by the seat of your pants and work entirely intuitively. You may never have made up a groundplan and may have no idea where to place the furniture or know the most effective ways to stage your actors. Don't worry about any of that. The idea is to acquire some experience of directing first, however primitively, so that when the technicalities of the craft come to the fore, you will have a frame of reference for them. Treat these initial exercises as would someone who wants to paint but is starting out with a sketch pad before creating his masterpiece.

Eventually we will use other actors to play ourselves and other people in events that we have chosen to put onto the stage, depending on the specific nature of the exercise. But first we are going to go on stage, solo.

Autorama Exercise

This is an exercise that I developed some years ago working with actors. It was designed to let the actor dip into feelings and experiences that are personal but artistically useful. It's really a way of saying, "Hey, use yourself in your work." It can be a useful exercise for directors who tend to think that personal exploration is only for actors and writers.

Perform a one-person show of the high points of your life in ten minutes. It must have the following qualifications:

1. It must be personal. Get to scenes, moments, events in your life that have been important and meaningful. If there are

areas that are very painful for you, don't go near them. This isn't psychodrama. If, however, an area is emotionally difficult but also one that you want to explore, try it.

2. It must be theatrical. Rather than standing there and telling us, "Now this happened to me . . .," find a metaphor or a frame for your presentation. One woman had been waiting on tables for so long that she felt her whole life was working in a restaurant. Her presentation was done serving imaginary customers at various tables. She served the doctor who delivered her, she ran between the tables that her divorced parents sat at, she served different food to different friends, she served huge platters of food to her bill collectors and kept auditioning for producers as she took their orders.

You can use lights, sound, video, other people in small parts if necessary; you can make it as complex or as simple as you like. It can be scripted or improvised. You can stop and refer to notes or have the whole thing memorized. Try to keep it no longer than ten minutes. Otherwise, it will ramble and become incoherent.

QUESTIONS AND ANSWERS

Q: I love playwrights. Why am I telling my own story?

A: Who's a playwright you love?

Q: Eugene O'Neill. *Long Day's Journey into Night*. Why can't I do a scene from that play?

A: Maybe you will. Whose story do you relate to more intensely: yours or the characters' in *Long Day's Journey?*

Q: Mine, obviously.

A: I'm asking you to put what you are most connected to onto the stage first. I'm asking you to explore parts of your life and present those parts with a certain degree of invention. When you work on *Long Day's Journey*, which is a very powerful and personal play, you are going to have to use many parts of yourself. You are going to have to touch areas that are profoundly painful. You may not have had a mother who was a morphine addict like Mary Tyrone or a father or brother who were alcoholic or a young brother who was tubercular, but you have to find what is universal in the experience of the Tyrones: what is being shared from their human condition to yours and hence to the audience's. If you don't want to learn how to use yourself, to exploit your own story so that you can connect with all kinds of material, you might just want to do a kind of theatre that is easy, ornamental, safe, or like television, totally comforting for the audience. This isn't to diminish you or that kind of work. But if you mention *Long Day's Journey into Night*, I'm assuming that you like to swim in more dangerous waters.

Q: What if the class doesn't like what I've chosen to do?

A: Good question. The atmosphere should be protective, and people have to trust each other. In other words, what is said and done inside the classroom has to remain there. What is revealed is not to be the cause of gossip. The question of "like" shouldn't exist. When you finish your autodrama people shouldn't feel obliged to like you, or to run up to you and say, "What a wonderful person you are." Nor should they compliment you on the cleverness of your presentation. "Your use of sound effects was dazzling!" Value judgments should be left at the door.

Q: I'll try it, but in the real world isn't it better that the director keeps his own feelings out of it and lets the actors do all the emotional stuff? All this "relating" and "connecting" and "use of self" is not what directing is about, is it? I mean, what about intellect and conceptualizing and interpretation of meaning? That's directing, isn't it?

A: Why it is that young directors who want everyone around them to be flexible to their ideas are often totally rigid themselves?

Some Results

Among the students in the class are a young man, Ted, and a young woman, Bette. He loves show business and musical comedy and believes that the sole purpose of theatre is entertainment. Bette, on the other hand, is very political and would like to see theatre advocate some of her pet social causes.

Ted's autodrama consisted of playing his life as a song-and-dance man. He wore tap shoes, a top hat, tails, and a cane. He danced his way through his own birth, through his difficult childhood; tapped his way through high school and sang songs about always falling in love with the wrong person; and when his mother died, he expressed it as Judy Garland singing "Over the Rainbow" and ended with a medley of torch songs about a life full of unrequited love.

The class felt that it took a great deal of courage for Ted to reveal himself in this way. What he showed was how he covers his feelings so that he won't be more vulnerable than he is. And when he does feel something intensely, such as falling in love with the "wrong" person, he has a genuine need to sing about it.

Bette's piece began with her playing with a ball, which represented her childhood. She then played with different balls, became very interested in some and discarded others: These were relationships. She became very attached to one ball that seemed to be her career, but others began to pull her away. She spent time juggling all the balls, and suddenly a small ball appeared. This seemed to indicate that she had a child. She tried to juggle all the balls again—baby, career, family, other interests—then threw them all into the air and let them fall where they would.

The class was surprised to learn all this about Bette. When asked how she felt doing it, she said, "Good. I hated to do this exercise, but I'm now wondering if I couldn't turn it into a half-hour performance piece."

FREQUENTLY ASKED QUESTIONS

Q: I was hoping that we'd get right into scene work and staging. I want you to teach me how to direct. How long do I have to wait?

A: No one can teach you how to direct. You have to have the opportunities to teach yourself, which is what we're doing.

Q: I'm worried that my instincts aren't worth anything, that directing is all an intellectual exercise for me, and maybe I've made a mistake going into this.

A: There's no sense giving up before you've begun. I don't think you should put a price on your instincts, such as they're worth nothing or a million dollars. I encourage you to explore your intuitive side and be able to express the things you have lived through in your work.

Q: When you direct is this what happens to you?

A: Yes. I see myself on stage no matter what the play is because I have related to it through facets of my own life experience, I have been guided by an inner voice, which is my intuition, and have staged the play from the fantasies of my own imagination.

Q: It sounds like what you've put on the stage is a reflection of yourself. Is that directing?

A: As I do it, yes. As it works for me, yes. As others do it or you do it, I can't say.

Q: So maybe I'll do it some other way?

A: Absolutely. But you're with me for now.

CHAPTER TWO

SUSTAINING DRAMATIC TENSION AND GUIDELINES ON CRITIQUING

DRAMATIC TENSION

In the first chapter we suggested that the core of directing is telling the story. Essentially a play works on many different story levels — narrative, emotional, psychological, social, symbolic, and so forth — and the director's job is to illuminate all those levels. A story is invariably held together by dramatic tension. This is the glue that binds the elements of a play, a novel, or a film: What will happen next, how will it all turn out, who did it, why did he do it, who's hiding in the darkness, is she safe, does he know he's in danger, who is going to win, and so forth? Dramatic tension is an important part of comedy as well. Will she get out the this jam? What if her husband finds out? His servant passed on the wrong letter, what now? How is this story ever going to unravel?

When you hear coughs coming from the audience, hear the rustling of programs, sense a general restlessness, or observe audience members looking at their watches, you have to know that you have not stretched the dramatic tension tight enough and that the only suspense that the audience is in is when it is going to be able to go home.

Tension doesn't always mean that the audience has to be in high suspense. Not every moment can be a cliff-hanger. But there has to be enough dramatic tension to compel the audience's interest throughout.

You might ask, "What story am I telling? The author is telling the story. Don't look at me for something he should have provided." It's true that the author has told a story. But the story he's told is on the page. The director's story is the one that is on the stage. Story awareness is important because a director can become so involved in the externals of production that no story is being told at all. Or a story is being told but sporadically, or without interest, or in a general and unspecific way.

Personal Stories

Before dealing with fictional material, let's go back to areas of personal experience. Take a situation from your own life that has occurred to you recently and look at it from a point of view of how much dramatic tension was in it. It doesn't have to be a major event such as a huge argument or an act of violence. It could have been quiet and subtle. Look back on the situation and examine it for:

What did you want?

What did another person or persons want?

What was the conflict?

Keep what you think you wanted and what the other person wanted simple. Don't convolute the circumstances. And keeping it simple, not overintellectualizing, is often the hardest thing to do for anyone who wants to direct. There is a mistaken notion of "If I want to direct I have to be smarter than everyone else. In order to be smarter, I must see more to any situation than anyone else. In order to see more, I have to find complex reasons for everything." Therefore, it's not uncommon to hear this kind of explanation when asked about a simple motive: "I wanted to break the psycho-symptomatic and Oedipal rivalry I have felt toward members of my dysfunctional family."

Always when you are trying to analyze "What did I want?" in a given situation, try to define it in one sentence. "I wanted to impress him that I would be great for the job." "I wanted to make her happy."

As a rule, stay away from words that temper or qualify your intentions. Often you will hear this kind of explanation: "Well, I kind of wanted to make her happy. I wanted to end the relationship, sort of." There can be no "kind of," "sort of" about it. Train yourself to be definitive, not vague. When you start working with actors and helping them with what they are playing you can't say of the character, "She kind of wants." Characters are not written in such a wishy-washy way. Temporizing is also a cop-out. It enables the director not to make a decision and stand by it. A director has to be fully committed to a choice until that choice is discarded for another.

Exercise

Working either with actors or members of your class do a ten-minute scene based on a recent event in your life that contained dramatic tension. You direct the scene. Another person will play you. (Many times people cannot give up the role that they played in their own situation and have to put themselves into their scenes, which is all right, but you're better off watching how the whole piece fits together from the outside. You can never get that perspective if you are still inside your own life.) It is important that you add to the mix what you wanted, what others wanted, and what the conflict was.

In the execution of the scene observe the following:

1. It will be impossible to redo the scene exactly as it happened in life, therefore, you should feel free to theatricalize it. You can bend time, you can heighten reality, and you can do and say things that were not exactly done and said at the time. In other words, you can "tweak" the actual event for theatrical effect or begin to fictionalize the situation.
2. It is very important that you don't use too many words. Don't feel that you have to do a lot of playwriting in that regard. You want to begin to find a visual language for working as a director. Think of this assignment as a silent film or a series of photographs that tell a story with as few words as possible.

The aim of the exercise is to synthesize some of the areas we've been discussing:

- Using our lives as material to explore.
- Putting that material onto the stage in theatrical ways.
- From our own stories we begin to see what a story is, how it happened, how it can be told.
- Tension is a key to storytelling and keeping the audience gripped.
- We are beginning to see storytelling in two ways: through words and through visualization.
- Working instinctively.

An Example

Ted and Bette, the two students who were always disagreeing with each other, decided to team up and do their tension exercise together. Their very opposing views on theatre, directing, and everything else were the basis of their scene, which took everyone by surprise because it began as an argument just as class began. They were sitting in their chairs, and we heard a loud discussion going on. The discussion became passionate and seemed quite real.

Ted: Well, why do you want to direct? To change the world?

Bette: I want the theatre to mean something to people. I want to say things about life today and how we need change in this country!

Ted: You're a director, not a sociologist.

Bette: The theatre can change our lives!

Ted: The purpose of the theatre is to entertain.

Bette: Like those silly musicals you're always talking about!

Ted: They're not silly, they're wonderful.

Bette: They're junk. They're adolescent!

Ted: Your ideas are junk, they're old-fashioned social realism.

Bette: You're a fool.

Ted: You're a fool.

Bette: You're stupid and vicious and mean.

Ted: You're pretentious, derivative, and boring! You're insane.

Bette: How dare you call me insane. Take that back.

Ted: You're not only insane, you're an idiot!

At that point Bette slapped Ted hard in the face. Several members of the class rose. Suddenly she pushed Ted, and he threw her across the room. One of the students in the class went to restrain him, but he broke loose and tackled Bette, who kicked him. Everyone looked to the teacher to stop this, but he stood along the wall of the class, smiling broadly. We understood from his reaction that none of this was real, that Ted and Bette were acting out their tension scene.

Bette took out a revolver and fired at Ted. He clutched his stomach, and suddenly blood was all over his hands and body. He fell back, writhing in pain, and took out his gun and shot Bette in the leg.

She bled profusely. They crawled like wounded animals to various parts of the room, leaving a trail of blood everywhere. Together they said, "Scene." Everyone applauded with gusto.

CRITIQUING

It is essential that anyone studying directing be able to critique the work of others in a very cogent and succinct way. Critiquing, however, has become something of a problem recently. People don't like to do it. You'll hear statements such as:

"I loved it. It was wonderful."

"I don't feel I should be negative."

"Isn't it more important to be supportive and nurturing? After all, we're all here to learn."

"I don't want to contribute to a mean-spirited atmosphere."

When you add that kind of thinking to the fact that so many students start to cry publicly or become humiliated or defensive during their critique, you begin to see how difficult a problem it can be.

Directing is a constant trial-and-error attempt to make all parts of the show work. We have to know when something is working and the reasons why! We have to be able to see when something is not working and know how to fix it. If you have been able to critique the work of others in an objective and effective way, you will be able to critique yourself.

Receiving the Critique

The following are advisable:

1. Shut up. Don't defend yourself. The audience either got it or didn't. If it didn't you have to find out why. Be quiet. Listening will only help you.

2. Take notes. Try to ascertain what each person is talking about. You may be nervous and unable to digest what is being presently said because you have a lot of noise in your head at the time. As you look your notes over later, they will be much

clearer to you. Also you may find that contradictory things were said. That's okay. You have to accept that. Sometimes contradictory points of view are really saying the same thing. One person may say that your scene was too slow, and the other may say that it went by too fast. It's possible that the rhythm and tempo you played the scene in need to be corrected.

Often what is said to you may be a symptom of something else. For example, someone tells you that the third act doesn't work. You know perfectly well that it works like a charm. What in the world can that remark, "The third act doesn't work," mean? Finally you come to realize that there is something wrong in the last half of the second act. You change that, get it to work better, leave the third act alone, and when the person comes back you'll hear, "The work you did on the third act is terrific!"

3. Always keep your ego out of the critique. It is not about you, it is about your work and your desire to grow, learn, and become a good director. You have to take whatever is said, pick yourself up, and start over again. This starts in class and continues through one's professional life. Having gotten past your own ego, you will find some of the criticism useful and will want to apply it to the next time you do the scene. Or use it as a helpful hint the next time out.

Giving the Critique

Your aim is to locate what didn't work and why. If you don't know why, just state "such and such did not work for me." More specifically, verbalize what was not clear or was confusing to you.

1. If there were things in the presentation you did not understand, cite what they were. I was once questioned after a preview about why a certain song was being sung at the end of the play. The person understood why the song was there, but it turned out that she did not know "why that particular song." I realized that her question was very important. The character was singing the wrong song! I

went to the theatre and changed it, and it made a great difference to the show. Comments questioning the reason for things are invaluable.

When the audience tells you that there is something it does not understand, it is really telling you that you have not dealt with what you've put before it, that you have not fulfilled the journey you're taking it on.

2. Don't hem and haw and talk circuitously or obliquely. Say what is on your mind. Being kind is not being truthful. Avoid palliatives such as, "It was great, I loved it, but . . ." You never have to be politic. You have to be only honest and to the point.

3. Don't join the cultural police. More and more students watch a scene and when asked to comment say, "I was offended!" Everything offends someone these days. When you ask what the director did that was so offensive the answer is usually, "His view of women is disgusting!" or "Even though you're a minority, what you're saying about your own people is terrible." Critiquing is not a forum for repressing the academic freedom of others.

4. Approach your criticisms from your sense of what the director was trying to achieve. Don't pitch a whole different approach to the work. The critique is not for you to display what you would have done or how you would go about doing it now. It's about what another person's work is and how you can help it.

You are training yourself to develop a very important skill: locating problems and solving them. Hence, you are always matching your work, your problems, your progress against the work, problems, and progress of everyone else. When you begin to see the reasons why something failed, how it was corrected and finally succeeded, you will begin to see what works and what doesn't work in the pieces you are observing as well as in your own. Students sometimes ask, "How will I know when something works or not?" It's like a musician asking, "How will I know when I make music?" All I can say is that something works when it feels right to me, when the pieces fit together and flow. When it lives.

The Critique of Ted and Bette's Tension Scene

Members of the class made the following comments:

- Some class members felt that the scene began unexpectedly as a conflict of ideas that got out of hand. The use of physical violence, although it was fun, seemed pasted on for the sake of itself.
- Others felt that the violence was more interesting than the debate of ideas.
- Some felt that after they got onto the scene, they saw how manipulative it was, that the directorial engineering was done for the sake of the exercise and in no way was organic.
- But others forgave its arbitrariness because they were held by the sustained dramatic tension throughout.
- Someone commented that she couldn't believe that sane men and women would behave like that. Others disagreed.
- Someone said that the scene was about fulfilling the exercise. Shouldn't a scene be about more than that?

At that remark Ted and Bette were asked what they were aiming for. The codirectors disagreed even about their joint venture. Ted wanted to do something shocking and take the audience off guard. Bette said she was aiming for more than that. She wanted to show how violence can erupt when two people are intolerant of each other's ideas.

What became clear was how Ted and Bette were not on the same wavelength and how that can weaken a collaboration.

Moreover, these questions arise: Should an exercise be more than an exercise, or should we, as directors, inject something more into it? Should the overall scene be about something? It was apparent that Ted and Bette, having conflicting ideas about what their scene was about, caused confusion for the audience. Even though, until now, we hadn't been dealing with that question, perhaps we'd better begin to.

The director's job is to ferret out and illuminate the meaning of the play. What is the scene about, the act about, the character about, the play about? These are the questions always in back of the director's mind. These, however, are more than just questions. They are the first principles of work that focuses us on our task. With that said, no matter what the exercise or text we are directing, we need to make it about something .

If we know what we're trying to reveal—what worked, what didn't work, and why it didn't—we will have the beginnings of directorial technique.

FREQUENTLY ASKED QUESTIONS

Q: How do we get to what a play is about?

A: Hopefully the ensuing chapters and techniques will help you. But you see how you have to work off your instincts, your life experience, and your research all at once. Asking how you get to know what a play is about is like asking what is life about: There are no easy answers. I can tell you what I think a particular play is about, and it very well could make no sense to you. You could see my production and say, "Ah, so that's what you thought that play was about! Well, I disagree." And I would say to you, "That's all right. Maybe when you do your production, I'll learn from your interpretation. However, even though we are divided on meaning, what did you think of the work you saw on the stage?" If you tell me that you thought it was well done and had its own integrity, I'd be very happy.

Q: You've emphasized simplicity. Is that a rule?

A: It is for me. The challenge in any art is to be simple. Bold, effective strokes are better than lots of complicated clutter. Simplicity is very hard. Complexity is easy, obfuscation is a snap, vagueness you can have by the yard. Getting to an essence is very, very difficult.

Q: How free are we when doing exercises from our life that contain dramatic tension?

A: You're as free as you want to be. You can take great liberties with actual events. Just keep the following: what you want, what the other person wants, and how that develops into conflict.

Q: What if I have something in mind, but there's not much dramatic tension to it?

A: Then you have to add it to the mix. These aren't observation exercises. These are experiences that have happened to you. The one thing to keep in the back of your mind is that they have to be stageworthy. If the actual scene wasn't, make it so. Or find an experience that was.

Q: But the stageworthiness of the scene shouldn't be forced, gratuitous, or arbitrary, like the one Ted and Bette did.

A: That's right.

Q: This is getting very hard. Simplicity, yet stageworthy. Personal, yet dramatic. Tension, yet not forced. And about something as well! How do you do it?

A: You mean, how do *you* do it?

CHAPTER THREE

EXTENDING OUR STORYTELLING RANGE AND FINDING VISUAL IMAGES

EXERCISE: "HOW I SPENT MY _____ VACATION"

Take notes on what you did during your last vacation—Christmas, summer, spring break, Labor Day weekend, and so forth. What happened? Who were you involved with? What incidents occurred? Use props, actors, yourself if necessary, sound effects, lights as needed. This piece is to be no more than fifteen minutes. You can script it, or you can work it out improvisationally with the actors. But it must have a beginning, middle, and end. In other words, not only is this exercise an extension of our previous work, but also it is suggesting that you give your story a certain form: It starts from a certain place you choose, it develops, and it concludes.

We are building upon the following:

Using autobiographical material to tell a story.

Finding ways of sustaining dramatic tension.

Thinking less in terms of words and more in terms of expressing our story visually.

Giving a more definite shape to our story.

Hoping to find through working what the experience was or what the story that we are telling is essentially about.

I want to trace how one student, John W., progressed within this assignment for several reasons. To begin with he did three versions of it. Each time he made a presentation, he was critiqued, redid his work, and presented it again. One would think, "This is nothing new, this is what we do. We try something, see what it's like, and redo it." Someone once asked Jerome Robbins during a rehearsal after a preview, "What are we doing today, Mr. Robbins?" He answered, "We are going to fix ten things!" There are students who never want to fix their work. They either say, "Tell me how I should do it" or they give up, saying, "Can't I go on to another scene?" No one can tell you how you should fix your exercise, your scene, your show. Once others start fixing it for you, it is no longer your show. You have abrogated your instincts for theirs, and they, in effect, have become ghost directors of what is supposed to be your work. The teacher or another student may have some specific reasons why what you've done doesn't work, what needs to be emphasized or rethought, but the solution—the "how"—has to be found by you because it's your work.

The attitude of not wanting to solve the problems that you yourself have laid out in the work that you've presented and instead wanting to move on to something else can lead to very bad habits. You have to be ferociously tenacious in your desire to "get it right," to say, "I am going to work on this piece until hell freezes over, but it's going to work!"

Wanting others to do the work for you or giving up is not where it's at—in directing, in art, in life.

JOHN W.'S "HOW I SPENT MY THANKSGIVING VACATION" PROJECT*

John W. based his piece on his Thanksgiving vacation when he couldn't go home and was stuck in town. He was bored and restless and called a few friends with the idea of doing something. He and his friends loved to play pool. He got one of them to play with him. John fancied himself a very good player, and after he and his friend began to play, he started feeling very confident and began betting: loser pays for beers, loser pays for hotdogs, loser pays for pool time, and so forth. What attracted John to the story were not only the events of what happened to him, but also the opportunity to express movement, body language, and the dynamics of shooting pool.

*Presented with permission of John Wray, the basis of whose project is herein used.

He placed a cube downstage-right and a cube downstage-left. Each area became a place for making phone calls between John and his friends. The pool table was made by putting two mats on top of two rectangular boxes. In the rear was a table used to set the cues and beverages.

The Use of Blackouts

It's important to note that John used blackouts a great deal. Whenever an episode was over, the lights went out. When the lights came back on we were usually in another time sequence. For example, even though we were in one pool game, the blackout gave the feeling that we were jump-cutting to various high points within that game. Sometimes the blackouts had the effect of many games having been played.

Blackouts have many uses. They make a strong statement, create a certain style, and serve as punctuation. But having a blackout while actors are scrambling into new positions or while furniture is being moved is cumbersome and can make an audience very uncomfortable as it sits in the dark, wondering when things will begin again. However, an effective blackout will help get a laugh and be timed so that just as the laugh is dying down, the action is ready to resume as the lights come up again. An effective blackout punctuates what the audience has just seen. It puts an exclamation point on the sequence. In musicals you will hear talk about "a button" on the end of a musical number. A button is a finish that helps gets the applause. There is a musical button, and there is a visual one as well. Usually the lights bump up at the end of a musical number, giving the audience a sense of an upbeat finish. A blackout is the opposite, but it is a button nevertheless.

Scenario 1

Lights come up, and John is seated on the cube down right, holding a phone and making dialing sounds. His friend Chris is seated on the cube down left, picks up the phone, and they begin a conversation that establishes the fact that Chris is busy, can't go out, but maybe Chris's roommate Jeff can. Jeff gets on the phone, and it's decided that he and John will shoot some pool.

Blackout.

When the lights come up Jeff and John each have a cue and are seriously studying the pool table. They decide that the game will be eight ball. Whoever wins will buy hotdogs from the bar. Because they are both actors they also decide that whoever gets a ball in a pocket will choose what dialect they are to speak in. They start with Scottish. As soon as John breaks, there is a blackout. (The billiard balls are imaginary.)

There follows a series of vignettes and blackouts. Each player leads with a different dialect, which means they are playing a fairly equal game.

At one point, John drops the eight ball into a pocket and loses the game. He announces, "Double or nothing."

John begins losing badly. He wants to play for "quadruple or nothing." As Jeff makes his final shot, John tries to blow his ball away from the pocket, but it succeeds in falling in. Jeff wins.

Blackout.

Back at his cube, John calls Chris to play pool with him. They arrange to meet.

In another series of shots done by vignettes and blackouts, John is winning. The boys decide to play for money, and John immediately begins losing. In the same cycle of bets and shots, John loses very badly to Chris, who by this time is eating dozens of hotdogs that John has had to pay for.

Blackout.

Lights up. John is curled up under the pool table, facing upstage in a fetal position, hugging his cue in humiliation. He is rocking back and forth and mumbling. Chris sits Indian-style upstage and lights a cigarette. Chris says, "John? John, come out from under the table, man." John doesn't move. Chris tries to convince John to stop playing pool because he already owes Chris a lot of money. John moans, "Dodecahedratuple or nothing." Chris says there's no such thing, but John wants one more game.

Blackout. Phone conversation.

John asks Chris to wait a few days before cashing his check.

Critique 1

The class was very excited about this scene because it had a strong, funny story that was very compelling. Because there was always something at stake the story progressed with a strong sense of dramatic tension. The moves that the actors made around the table using their cues and playing imaginary pool were fluid, varied, and had the smell of truth about what goes on during a game. (It was also a relief to see a scene that didn't take place in a living room for a change.)

Several questions did arise, however.

Although the image of John cowering under the table like a junkie begging for one more fix was funny and arresting, it seemed to come from nowhere. I, as the teacher, thought it was effective and imaginative. It worked for me. And I thought the class was being a little too literal-minded in not appreciating it. Yet, in another way, I could see what was bothering the class. The image was not quite earned. This means that it was theatrically effective, but it really did not come from an organic source: It was a wonderful idea, tacked on for the sake of its theatrics. Nothing really led up to it. We did not see a man driven to such desperate behavior.

The other criticism that the class had was that John's friends came off like pool sharks. The class saw John as a sucker being hustled by better players. This was not John's intention at all. So it became very clear that the first thing the director had to do was make his leading character more active. John wanted to play, he had great confidence in his skills, he was totally deluded about his chances, and he could never give up in spite of all reality.

The points made in a critique will often lead to a pattern or a certain picture. Seemingly disparate comments, when put together, all work together. In this case, John's passivity was the reason why the wonderful image of him under the pool table did not work for the class. If he had been strong enough, had been pursuing his need to win with a real mania and obsession, his falling to his knees and cringing in a rage under the table, begging for one more game, would have been that word again: *organic*. In other words, it did not spring naturally from the moment.

My suggestion to John was to try to slow the whole scene down. The dialects were not clear nor was the reason why the actors were speaking in them. Not wanting to stifle his imagination by harping on the image of him under the table I suggested that he find more images like that. In short, he needed to deepen his character's obsession for winning and take it as far as it will go. One of the keys to directing is to take your ideas as far as they will go. Never go for what's safe, comforting for the audience, or easy to watch. If you have an idea, go the distance with it. This is what makes theatre alive and exciting.

Scenario 2

John reworked his scene. In his notes he wrote: "I want to try to focus on the mania of John's gambling compulsion. I don't think I have to be so literal. In other words, John's mental state is such that all sorts of theatrical things can happen. I want to start the scene realistically, then get very wild with it. Mainly, I want to take my ideas as far as they will go. (This is going to take more courage than I may have.)"

John used the same groundplan, slightly altering the setup of the opening phone call. He made his own character more positive: that is, he did not set himself up as a loser right from the start.

The pool game proceeded at a slower pace, and the change of dialects was clearer. He slowly began to lose, and the more he lost, the more he bet. His friend Jeff succeeded in making one incredible shot after another. John's jealousy and frustration were more clearly defined.

Although the outline of the story proceeded in the same way as the first scenario, John found two very striking physical images. After one blackout the lights came up, his friend made a spectacular shot, and John fainted on top of the pool table, the cue coming out of his chest as though he'd been shot down like a defenseless deer.

After a series of shots in which his friend was playing almost superhuman pool, there was a blackout. The lights came up, and John was standing on the upstage table, his shirt around his waist like a loincloth, his arms wrapped around the cue like a crucifix, and the rack triangle around his head like a crown of thorns.

After this there was a blackout, a few more shots, and the image of John under the pool table again.

The scene resolved itself with a telephone call, John asking his friend to delay cashing his check.

Critique 2

There was a general sense of satisfaction and admiration for the way John was working. He was improving his scene and finding vivid, funny, and very telling physical images along the way. All his images were connected to being persecuted, slain, mortally defeated, which had to do with his gambling mania. The scene got to be about how he dramatizes himself when he loses. He probably wouldn't be half as interesting to himself if he won.

My suggestion was that the images might be routined in a different way. That is, presented in a different order. The crucifixion was such a high point that it was almost the button on the experience. Nothing could follow it. It was like having your best joke followed by a weaker one. You save your best joke for last, then get off the stage. The image of being under the table lost all effect because it had to follow the crucifixion.

Conclusion

John redid this scene a second time and presented it to a public audience when we brought together the best work of the group into an evening's event. He made the scene sharper by using fewer dialects and gave his characters more detail. I would like to report that he took my advice and held off the crucifix image until the end of the pool hall sequence, but he did not. I can report only that the image got such a huge response that nothing seemed as effective afterward. It was like being at the musical *Gypsy*, doing "Rose's Turn," that great epic eleven o'clock number written for Ethel Merman to close the show, and trying to follow it with something else.

John W.'s Notes on His
Experience with This Assignment

"I learned that even seemingly boring events can be theatrical. But as soon as I looked into the gambling obsession and the bizarre theatrics of the scene, I got excited about staging it.

"I learned how easy it is to unintentionally make a main character passive (especially if the piece is autobiographical). First, I think there's a tendency to make weak dramatic choices because we want to make ourselves likable or to come off like the martyr or the good guy. In reality our motivations are just as selfish and manipulative as everyone else's. Secondly, I think we lose a certain objectivity when we examine ourselves.

"I learned how powerful blackouts can be. Almost anything becomes funny with a well-timed blackout, and blackouts can let you get away with murder. I think it's the equivalent of walking out of a joke. If you hit the joke and run or move away, it's a lot funnier than if you stand there waiting for the laugh. I found that if I lingered on the image too long I would lose the joke. I had to find the timing: how long to stay on the image and just when to black out. It was all basic instinct but seemed to work in the end.

"I mainly learned that there is no such thing as going too far. Or if there is, the line is much further out there than we all think it is. The real danger isn't taking something far enough; so it's usually a good idea to try to take it further no matter what."

GETTING MORE VISUALLY ORIENTED

Some students appreciate the visual skills in others but seem to be unable to find images in their own work. Their exercises remain largely static, and their characters become talking heads. One good way of telling if a story is being told visually is to "turn the sound off," that is, have the actors do the scene without speaking. Just let them go through their staging. If a story is not being told by how they are moving, you have to know that a story is not being told at all. Unless it's a Samuel Beckett play that is designed for words and no movement (and the lack of movement is a major story point), you know that you are relying too heavily on words.

Even though we are not into the details of staging yet, know that your story has to be visually as well as verbally expressed.

Rent some silent films and observe how complex, intriguing stories were told with no dialogue. Rent one of your favorite recent movies, turn the sound off, and see how much of the story was told just by its visuals.

The following exercise is designed for you to do an extended exercise such as "How I Spent My _____ Vacation," but to present it as though you were a photographer and took a dozen snapshots of the high points of the story.

Exercise: A Story Told in Freeze-Frames

Work the story out with your actors, knowing that you are going to present twelve tableaux, or twelve still pictures, using them to tell the story. Start with a blackout, get your actors in place, bring up the lights for your first picture. No words, no action, no movement. Blackout. Go into the second image. Do this a dozen times and see if the audience got the gist of your story. In a way it's not important that the audience understood your story fully. It's important that you have opened yourself to working like this. Go back and present your story any way you like, but incorporate the images that you thought were the most successful. When you read a play, you will always see certain images that are important to you and will try to engineer the action into the images.

Exercise: Staging Dreams

So far the discussion has been about autobiographical stories that are essentially literal and logical. An interesting exercise is to stage a dream. Dreams are nonliteral, but highly imagistic. Recall a dream, using actors and props, and represent it on stage. You will find that you will be working much more freely in terms of visualization. You won't have to bother making narrative sense because many dreams don't. And as far as what the dream meant, if your images are strong enough, each audience member will have his or her own interpretation.

CHECKLIST

As you are doing your assignments, consider the following:

1. Do my blackouts work? Can I live without them? Do I have too many? Is there too much scrambling in the dark? Are they becoming predictable? If so, can I make them happen at more unexpected spots? Is every vignette of equal length, thereby losing surprise for the audience?

2. I have some very theatrical moments. Are they earned? Do they come from an organic center? Are they really revealing the truth of the situation, or are they arbitrary and done for the sake of themselves?

3. Are my central characters working out of the positive? Are they fully playing what they want, or are they attitudinizing, such as trying to come across as having general qualities like being nice, being a victim, being sympathetic? Is the pursuit of the objective being played like the characters really want something? Is there something at stake for the characters?

4. Have I taken things far enough? Am I being timid, or can I push things further? Am I frightened to go the limit? I want the scene to have some edges, some bite, I want it to be hard and tough, but am I settling for being comfortable? Am I letting the audience off the hook by settling for less than I really want?

5. Am I trusting the actors and the story enough? Why am I pushing the pace so? Why don't I allow the moments to breathe? No one's going to run me out of town if I take five minutes more to let the piece unfold in a more natural pace and rhythm.

6. I've found some effective images. How can I find more? Am I relying on the words too much to do the work for me? What if I run the piece in silence, just to look at what it expresses visually? Why don't I do the exercise of trying to see what my visual high points are and see: (a) if I'm telling the story and (b) what other images will come to mind.

7. What if I did this whole piece as a dream? I could invent anything, really go the limit on being free, breaking out of my literal-minded box. After I've explored that way of working, I
   can put some of the dream images into my story, which is literal and sequential but which will be helped by images that
   came from this other source.

PART TWO

THE DIRECTOR AS INTERPRETER

Reading the text and questions that are helpful to ask about it.

Examining content and structure.

Evaluating the author's use of language and its effect on character.

Techniques for working with language.

CHAPTER FOUR

READING THE TEXT

By this time the student is anxious to direct a play. He feels that he has storytelling ability and is getting a feel for working visually. "So where are my actors, where's the stage, who's going to design the set? I'm ready!" When I was a student we immediately began with the fundamentals of staging: movement, picturization, composition, tempo, rhythm, and dynamics. As a result we knew how to stage a show fairly well without knowing what a story was. You may ask: If we weren't staging the story, what were we doing? We were doing movement, picturization, composition, and so forth like child prodigies who had great technical mastery but were nowhere near the meaning of the music.

The work that we have done so far has been to tell stories from our personal experience. We've bent reality and fictionalized for dramatic effect, but the stories were our own. Now it's time to enter the world of the playwright. He or she is telling a story. It's on the page. But the director, by lifting it off the page and putting on the stage, becomes a co-storyteller with the writer. Hopefully this means that you are telling the playwright's story with your directorial tools: staging, acting, production, and so forth. The ritual for the audience members of sitting in the dark, looking up at a stage, and watching actors portray characters who go through the life of a story is primarily why they've come to the theatre.

Before we start rushing into production, let's look at the way a director reads a text and what is looked for. Reading a play for the first time, I'm struck by its content, structure, meaning, style, and language. But I always ask four basic questions first:

1. What Is My Gut Response?

Many young directors believe that they have to respond to a play in a highly intellectual way. They view a play as something that they have to be very smart about, so that when they are talking about it, people will be impressed. They'll talk in terms of symbolism, metaphors, historical context, construction versus deconstruction, and so forth. All this isn't necessary. Not to begin with, at least. It's more important that you receive the play as a human experience, simply and intuitively: "I like it, I hate it, it's funny, it's moving, it has disturbed me, it's taken me places I've never been, it's been an adventure, a trip."

As a director, if I have a positive reaction, if I have enjoyed reading the play, I know I will be able to convey that pleasure to an audience. It's not a bad idea to write down your responses because those initial feelings can often get lost in the course of production. One day you'll look at a dress rehearsal and say, "This is the dreariest show I've ever seen. Whatever made me think I liked it?" Return to your notes, and you'll find how far you've strayed from your initial reactions, and hopefully you will recognize what you have to do to get them back. You might recall that you thought the play was very funny when you first read it. "So how come it looks like *King Lear* on a rainy day up there? I've lost all the absurdity and dynamics of a comedy. Everyone seems to be moaning around in the dark, and no one is pursuing anything."

If you have an antipathy toward a play and have the assignment of directing it, you have to find what is positive about it. Some of the best work I've ever done has been with material I initially did not care for; and some of the plays that I faltered on were the ones I loved to death.

You certainly have to read the play more than once. As you do you will appreciate its strengths, but you will also become aware of its weaknesses. Directing a play can't be an unabashed love affair where you are blind to its problems. Confront those problems with reality so that they will be solved by you with imagination and effort. Anyway, the problems with any play, any actor, any of the areas that the director works in should always be looked upon as a challenge.

2. What Is This Play About?

One of the many ways that the job of a director has been defined is as that of "interpreter." This means that the director is the person who holds the keys to what the play means and how that meaning should be presented. The director has unlocked the play, has decoded it, and has analyzed it in such a way that the audience will ultimately receive

its meaning. This is similar to what conductors do. A Brahms symphony is interpreted differently by Toscanini, Solti, Bernstein, and
Von Karajan. Each conductor sees it a different way. More precisely,
each hears it differently. The differences, however, are not done for
the sake of themselves or as conducting caprices. The differences are
fervently held passions about what each conductor believes the composer intended and how each note should be performed.

What the director believes the play to be about is the glue that
keeps everyone's work together. During preproduction and rehearsals
the director is asked a million questions. Each answer is informed by
what the director believes the play is about. "Do you like the set for
this scene?" "No. It's not what the scene is about, it's not what the play
is about." Knowing what the play is about is especially useful when
directing a new play. I once had an author who did a brilliant set of
rewrites. We were on the floor laughing; that's how wonderful the
material was. The actors loved it; the author couldn't be more pleased.
I took him aside and said, "These are wonderful pages, but for some
other play. They are not what your play is about." He looked at me and
in all sincerity asked, "What is my play about? I forgot!"

Unfortunately, a good play doesn't hit you over the head in the
first five minutes and scream, "I'm about so and so. Get it!" Part of
the fun of watching a good play is allowing it to take you to where it's
going, gently and subtly. Sometimes you think you know what a play
is about and find that it's about something else entirely after you
begin to rehearse it. I've had the misfortune of finally understanding
what a play was about as I watched it on my opening night—when it
was too late. It's also too late in mid-rehearsal because scenery and
costumes are being built, and they are not going to be changed unless
you have a very rich producer.

A director determines what the play is about largely from his
own investigations, but as he and his collaborators work, an evolution
takes place. The designers will come up with things you haven't realized before, the actors will bring to life scenes that open whole new
areas for you. You will see things in a new and richer light every
minute because working on a play is a living, growing, amazing experience. But all this evolving within the creative process should reinforce your beliefs. If they cause them to alter or completely change,
you can be open and say, "Hey, gang, remember everything I've said

about this play? Disregard it. I was wrong." As I said, this is costly not only financially, but also in terms of the trust that your collaborators have in you. You now are a person who changes his mind every week. If what you have determined the play is about is substantiated by the text, you are going to be on firm ground. This sounds almost too obvious, but there is a tendency, especially in college theatre, to run off and make the play about what the director's pet social or theatrical notions of the day are and not about what the author intended.

How Do You Begin to Decipher Meaning?

Go with your instincts and imagination. What is being suggested to you? How close do you feel to the situation, how removed? Do you begin to see any of these people? Do you have a glimmer of the world they are in? Is it like anything you know?

You will start to do research on the play, the author, the period, and so forth. You can also read commentaries and reviews of past productions to find out what others thought the play was about. I prefer not to do that at first. I want to make up my mind myself. It's only when I've got my own grasp on the material that ideas begin to flow for me. What the critic for the *New York Times* thought doesn't help me direct my production of the play.

But insights into the author, where the work fits into his or her oeuvre, and what was happening in the world when the play was written are links to its genesis and help one's comprehension enormously. If I'm doing a play by George Bernard Shaw and find that it was written at the precise time he was involved with Fabian Socialism in England, the overall idea of the play becomes clearer: I know where the characters are coming from and can understand the context of their debates with each other.

Write the story of the play in your own words because the idea of the play is told in its story. For example, Tennessee Williams's *A Streetcar Named Desire*. What that play is about is all in the story that it tells and the way it tells it. Blanche DuBois covers her past with lies and illusions in order to maintain her fragile sense of sanity and hope. When she's unmasked by her brother-in-law, Stanley Kowalski, she is unable to confront the truth, or more precisely, she is unable to live with the truth and steps into the refuge of insanity. Stanley provokes Blanche into a place she does not want to go—the truth. He rapes her and finally exposes her as a fraud and a liar. Her sister, Stella, is in the middle, torn between her loyalty to her husband and love of her sister, not knowing what is true and sometimes not wanting to know. The play, scene by scene, pivots on the truth. The play, through its monologues, goes back in time and through its action moves forward at the same time. Like a Greek tragedy it keeps digging into past events where truth is buried. But it moves forward in present time irrevocably until that truth about Blanche is revealed. Once the truth is revealed, the play is finally resolved.

Every character in a play has a particular function in the story and its overall intention. Every character is integral to what the play is about, even if it's a character who stands for the opposite of everything the author wants you to believe. Many Restoration comedies portrayed a very amoral world, but the portrayal didn't mean that the authors were advocating vice and venality. In David Mamet's *Sexual Perversity in Chicago*, one man has terrible misconceptions about women and is sexist in his views, almost to an absurdly funny degree. Mamet uses him to demonstrate a typical macho male who is incapable of having any kind of relationship with women and who uses his stories either to woo or abuse them, mainly to abuse them because he always sets himself up for rejection. He's a man who, for all his womanizing, hates women. People say, "I don't like Mamet's plays—he doesn't like women." This view completely misses the point.

In many of Shaw's plays he will present characters who have conflicting points of view, yet taken together they all are a part of one large, multifaceted argument leading to a particular point of view about how the world should evolve to a higher plane.

The characters in a Chekhov play are usually on a merry-go-round of unrequited love. In *The Sea Gull*, Medvedenko loves Masha, Masha loves Trepleff, Trepleff loves Nina, Nine falls in love with Trigorin, Trigorin loves himself. Set against this comic atmosphere where all this romantic pursuit is going on is another story. Each character swings back and forth between self-love and self-hatred, between being arrogant one moment and humiliated the next, feeling that he or she has the secret to life, to art, to the theatre on the one hand and feeling overwhelmed with worthlessness and despair five minutes later. The play is about the duality of our nature: how we can create or destroy depending on where our ego is when we choose to act. Every character's story portrays this idea.

3. How Do I Make the Play Happen Onstage?

Have you ever, when watching the production of a play, thought, "Why is nothing happening up there?" People are shouting, running around, in some cases killing one another, crying, repenting, hugging one another, and singing and dancing, but nothing is really happening! For all its activity the show remains dead. Everyone on stage is going through the externals of emotion and action, but nothing has happened that moves the inner core of the play. Tyrone Guthrie used to talk about the theatre as a great occasion. What he meant was that we go to it as something very special because it *is* special. It is an event. An *event* implies a happening. A *happening* implies something that is alive every second of its existence. People love to watch sports for this reason. The outcome of the game can hinge on seconds. There can be reversals, surprises, breath-stopping moments of suspense, unexpected moves, players whom you root for, and a result you either love or hate.

Explore the following as means of getting the play to happen:

Events (External and Internal).   Some plays have an external event as well as a series of internal events. These events propel the action. Now the word *action* can be used in many different ways. In acting terms it means what the character is doing to get what she wants. In dramatic terms Aristotle talked about a play as being "an imitation of an action." In film the director calls for "action" when the lights, camera, sound, and actors are ready to begin. For me, actions are the events, episodes, or incidents that happen onstage and that move the story and plot forward.

By the way, I just used two words that are often mistakenly used interchangeably: *story* and *plot*. *Story* is basically the simple outline of the play. *A Doll's House* is the story of a marriage that is held together by illusions and destroyed by reality. *Plot*, however, is the complex building of one incident upon the other. The play opens, and Nora enters with a porter who is carrying a Christmas tree. She puts her packages down and tips the porter, and he leaves. She secretly eats macaroons and is almost caught by husband Torvald, who enters and accuses her of being a spendthrift and so forth.

Back to events. Many plays are launched by something going on outside their interior. In Brecht's *Mother Courage* a long war is being waged. In Sean O'Casey's *Plough and the Stars* the Irish uprising is happening. In John Guare's *The House of Blue Leaves* the pope is about to visit New York City for the first time. These events dictate the behavior of the characters who play off of them. People complain that nothing happens in Chekhov, but what greater event and factor in how people behave than the impending loss of one's property, as in *The Cherry Orchard*? Unless the director and actors use the **external events** of the play as trigger mechanisms of character behavior and action, the play does not happen. These events always ante up the stakes for what the characters are pursuing, and that pursuit drives the action. As a matter of fact, the pursuit itself is very often the action. The external event of *Romeo and Juliet* is the blood feud between the Montagues and Capulets. Ironically, instead of this being an obstacle to Romeo and Juliet it eventually becomes a challenge to overcome. They are taboo to each other and consequently want each other more. The feud drives the play forward. The closer the lovers come to each other, the further apart they're driven by death, banishment, revenge, murder, and final irreconcilable tragedy.

Internal events are those moments that happen to the characters right on stage. They are usually caused by external circumstances, and the audience is witness to how the characters react to them for the first time. The balcony scene of *Romeo and Juliet*, act 2, scene 2, is a good example of "first timeness." There is a sense of discovery by each character about the other, neither of whom has ever experienced anything like what is happening now. The scene exists in the present tense. And the present tense is where the director always wants the work to be.

Romeo: But soft! what light through yonder window breaks?
It is the east, and Juliet is the sun! —
Arise, fair sun, and kill the envious moon,
Who is already sick and pale with grief,
That thou her maid art far more fair than she.

In just five lines, see how much is happening:

"But soft!" Romeo is quieting himself because he doesn't want to stop what he thinks is coming before him. He sees a light behind a window on the balcony. Suddenly Juliet enters. This is amazing for him. In his mind the garden is now lit up brilliantly even though it's still night. He sees Juliet as belonging to the sun: dazzling, radiant, the heat of love. The moon that thought she was so special is now diminished, envious that Juliet is brighter than she.

The specifics—his desire to encounter this girl, the need to turn his ardor into poetry, the impulsiveness of the life force running through him, and the need to make physical contact—all are events popping, one after the other, as the scene takes place.

In Juliet's "potion scene," in which she debates the pros and cons of consuming the vial that Friar Lawrence gave her, she conjures up what it would be like to be dead and be among the ghosts of her ancestors. Juliet finally does take the potion. But why? In most productions the actress rhapsodizes through this speech and finally drinks the contents of the vial. The director has to ask, "What happens within this speech to make Juliet drink?" Is there a specific event that is the trigger to her action? If so, what is it? Where is it? Is it something that happens in front of the audience? Some directors might decide, "She knows she's going to take the potion, she just has to argue her way through it because she's frightened." If so, that means that she has made her decision offstage and is using stage time to go through her dilemma. It's always more effective and immediate if characters go through their dilemma and find solutions with the audience present. (It's certainly more interesting for the audience.)

The internal event is among these lines:

Juliet: O, look! me thinks I see my cousin's ghost
       Seeking out Romeo, that did spit his body
       Upon a rapier's point: stay, Tybalt, stay!
       Romeo, I come! this do I drink to thee.

Juliet drinks the potion to protect Romeo from Tybalt's vengeance. That moment of knowing what she must do to protect Romeo is an internal event. It changes the course of the action for the character and for the rest of the play. It happens onstage and as a result creates suspense and dramatic tension for the audience.

Note: When I say that the present tense is where the director wants to be, the logical question is, "But what about all those speeches from the Greeks to Tennessee Williams that talk about past events, that go so back in time? The present seems lost." Those speeches are there for a particular reason. They are designed not only to inform us of the past, but also to move the play forward. You will notice that these speeches all have an internal event, which means that something happens to the character as a result of talking about the past or that something happens to the listener. Therefore, the speech does exist for the purpose of activating present-time action.

Recognitions.   In a Greek play a character might find a lock of hair on a rock and suddenly recognize it as belonging to her long-lost brother of twenty years ago. This was a big moment because the audience watched the character absorb a new piece of information, which the audience already knew. But watching the character get the information was a big event.

Recognitions take many different shapes, but they help the director shift the action, find another key to play the scene in, and help develop the story. They also happen onstage. One of the most famous recognitions is Oedipus's understanding that *he* is the man he has been pursuing as the cause of all the misery in Thebes. It is a moment that happens onstage. His perceiving who he really is and what he has done is a great theatrical moment because it is ignited before us. We have waited for it, and the playwright delivers it at last. We see the recognition sink in, we witness his suffering and become anxious about what he will do to himself.

If you go through the play that you are reading and examine how the author has laid out the various character recognitions, such as new insights, revelations, and understanding of the truth, you will have a good road map for making the play come to life.

Ibsen is loaded with very dramatic recognitions, the most famous of which is Nora's understanding in *A Doll's House* that she must leave. Action in that play is ever-changing because of the continually new information that the characters are getting and new ways they are receiving it.

For another example, Ibsen's Hedda Gabler is a character who is very quick to recognize who everyone around her is: She knows the truths and weaknesses about everyone. The great recognition in the play comes when she recognizes who *she* is: someone no one needs. And when she finally perceives that, she puts a bullet in her head.

Reversals.   Every good story twists and lands in unexpected ways. The Greeks often wrote about the reversal of fortune of great men who were kings and nobles and who fell from their lofty heights into suffering and tragedy. In the twentieth century writers reversed the idea of reversal: They took an everyman character who was essentially an underdog and dramatized how he went from being a loser to overcoming great odds.

Reversals are more than active plot points. They are events that keep the play alive. Ibsen in *A Doll's House* practically built the whole play on a series of reversals. Nora thinks she has saved her husband only to find out that what she has done was a terrible mistake. She tries to work herself out of the problem and to a certain extent believes that she is succeeding, but she and her husband are threatened with blackmail. The great reversal for Nora comes when she recognizes that her husband will not protect her and threatens to take the children away from her. But things turn again: The play seems to be on the verge of a happy ending when the blackmailer withdraws his threat. But Nora, understanding who her husband is and who she must try to become, leaves the marriage.

4. How Has the Play Been Put Together?

A play is like a symphony in certain ways. Themes are suggested, laid out, and then developed. There are contrasting ideas, unexpected colors, counterpoint, climaxes, resolutions, and a finale. Some symphonies are a coherent, organized whole, and others like to surprise you by veering off one way, then another, and to throw everything including the kitchen sink at you. A symphony is put together with mathematical precision. It is built purposefully and technically and supported with an inner architecture of its own.

A good play has a structure carefully designed to house the contents of its story. Taken together, that structure and its contents add up to the life of the play and its overall meaning. The director, by vivisecting the play's structure—that is, examining how that play has been put together—will get inside the play's essence and be able to convey it to the audience. A play can always be open to many interpretations—the definitive production of anything is very rare. The same director can go back to the same play ten years later and understand it in a completely different way, but he or she should be able to say, "When I rolled up my sleeves and dug into it, this is what I discovered at the time. . . ." Of course, after you begin to work with actors and explore every line and every moment, the structure of the play will come to light, but until then you want to find out as much as possible about the play yourself.

What do I mean by *structure*?

I've seen *structure* defined as "rising actions and falling actions" with charts and graphs and arrows pointing in different directions. I've seen needles showing climaxes and crises and secondary climaxes and double resolutions like a printout of a polygraph test. None of this helps me as a director because I have to answer certain questions about the play. If I can answer them, I can figure out how the play was put together.

- Why is this scene here, in this place, now?
- What is the overall purpose of this scene? Does it serve a particular function?
- Why is he entering now?
- Why does he stay onstage for the next five pages?
- What purpose is this character serving in the story?
- Why is this speech two pages long? Why at this spot? What is supposed to happen as a result of it?

Every play creates its own logic. And it's this logic that is part of the play's structure. That's why the more questions you ask of the play, the more you will fathom how it was made.

Other than its very own logic, a play has been constructed by the use of particular elements. Getting away from the lofty analogy of the symphony, think of soup. A soup is put together by the use of certain ingredients that determine its structure. Here are some of the ingredients, or elements, that can be used in a play. The way they are used, how they are parceled out, and to what degree are integral to the play's construction.

ELEMENTS OF STRUCTURE

Length.   Shakespeare spoke of "two hours traffic upon the stage."
I recently sat through an audition in which a young woman took
twenty minutes to do Nina's final speech in *The Sea Gull*, a speech
normally played in three or four minutes. "I'm a sea gull, no, I'm not.
I'm an actress." The monologue took on Robert Wilson proportions
where time is bent out of shape and the world is submerged into new-
found dimensions of boredom. In this play Chekhov knew that he
was at the end of a long four-act play. There are very few long
speeches. The dialogue is compact and terse. The three or four minutes that it should take is long by Chekhovian standards, but its
length is earned by the fact that it unravels the central drama of the
play, which is the paradox between self-hatred and self-love. Stage
time is precious. Waste it, and you've lost the audience. Length therefore is a strategic element of structure. The director and the author
have to know how long the audience will be compelled by what they
are presenting.

Edward Albee's *A Zoo Story* compresses a very volatile story into
one act—not much longer than a Greek play, as a matter of fact. The
play is linear and uncluttered by subplots. There is a unity of time,
place, and action. The action is cyclical: Jerry provokes Peter, who
responds. Jerry provokes Peter repeatedly until a crisis develops over
the bench. Jerry wants it. Peter won't give it up. Jerry pulls a knife,
drops it, urges Peter to pick it up, and the climax of the play is Jerry
impaling himself on the knife. The denouement or resolution is that
Jerry permits Peter to run off, avoiding any part in this.

The structure is built on fifty minutes or so of stage time.

Longer plays tend to have more plot, strands, themes, and ideas,
which take more time to develop and resolve.

Exposition.   In movies today we can sit through twenty minutes of violent action and not have the faintest idea why any of it
is happening. Taking "the ride" into special effects and visuals is
something we do without question. After awhile there will be a few
plot points and explanations to satisfy our demand to know a little
of what is going on. These movies invariably terminate in a huge
battle scene that pulls out all the stops and in which you never can

tell which side is which, but none of this makes a difference. The star is victorious, the couples are reunited, the enemies have been vanquished. The visual impact has seduced us.

Movies can, and do, live with very little exposition that requires words. (Words are not the movies' best friend.) Plays have to grip an audience in a different way. A story is being told by actors saying words, and the story usually begins with exposition that sets up the action that proceeds.

While two servants are setting up the room for a dinner party, they will be gossiping about the history of everyone coming that evening, who is who, where everyone has been, and the trouble the main characters are in.

Exposition is what Hollywood calls today "the back story." Some plays never stop with their exposition. Ibsen, for example, in both *A Doll's House* and *Hedda Gabler* keeps the back story going almost to the play's resolution. Tennessee Williams uses the same technique. The past becomes the key to all the questions we are tantalized with along the way. Bit by bit the back story unfolds until all our curiosity is satisfied: Was she a prostitute, what happened to cousin Sebastian that brought on her breakdown, why does he drink, what broke her heart, and so forth.

Since the end of World War II playwrights have found that by eliminating exposition, or eliminating as much as they can, a heightened aura of mystery and dramatic tension can be evoked. Pinter, for instance, in *The Birthday Party* has events taking place with no seeming reason and no background for them. Stanley is a lodger in a seaside rooming house. We know nothing about him except that he's a concert pianist who one day went to the concert hall and was locked out. Two men come to visit him and end up psychologically torturing him. Why? We don't know. We know practically nothing about them. There is no back story about their relationship to Stanley or what informs any of their actions. But its lack of information is what gives the play its power. The play leaves itself open to suggest whatever comes into our minds as we watch it. Its short two-act form creates inexplicable terror and foreboding for the audience. People are frightened, moved to tears, and filled with dread, and they don't know why. Or if they do know why, it's because they have filled the missing exposition with their own imagination or private experience.

In contrast, imagine if Ibsen had written this play. It would have been four acts long, and we would know everyone inside out. Most likely, however, he would have dispatched the entire story of *The Birthday Party* in two pages of exposition and would have gone on to how seaside resorts are being polluted.

Mystery.   Mystery is built by getting the audience members to want something and withholding it from them. The tease is to dole out information in small increments. Along the way the writer might throw out a certain amount of "misinformation." This is known as a red herring, which is a clue that leads you up the wrong alley.

Oedipus is built on solving a mystery. It is a great whodunit. Except that we know who did it from the start: Oedipus. The mystery for us is how will the information get to him, when will he recognize that he is the man, and what will he do?

Arthur Miller's *Death of a Salesman* builds a mystery around several questions: What has caused the disintegration of Biff? Why has he gone from a high school hero to a man in his thirties who is a petty thief and a failure? Why has he lost all respect for his father, Willy Loman? A pivotal incident is finally revealed. In a crisis because he failed an important exam that would have gotten him into college, Biff goes up to Boston to talk to his father about what to do. He catches Willy with a prostitute, paying her off with a pair of new stockings that was supposed to go to Biff's mother.

Cat on a Hot Tin Roof is built on the mystery of Maggie and Brick's sexual relationship and the more complex questions of Brick's alcoholism and whether or not he's homosexual. The playwright never really solved Maggie and Brick's relationship because there are at least three versions of the end of the play. Often the author poses a mystery, and the entire act of writing the play is for him a way to find out how it ends.

Cat on a Hot Tin Roof is built by probing the mystery of unanswered questions, such as:

Why do you hate me, Brick?

Why do you drink?

What was between you and Skipper?

Why don't you and Maggie have children?

Why don't you sleep with your wife?

Who are you leaving your money to, Big Daddy?

Argument.   From Sophocles's *Antigone* to David Mamet's *Oleanna*, argument is integral to the structure of plays. It's hard to think of a play where there is no argument. Argument is another way of expressing conflict, and theatre is dramatized conflict. An issue arises, sides are taken, and argument begins. It can take the form of a debate or outright warfare, but it is waged until there is some kind of reconciliation or resolution. It is an essential ingredient in a play's structure. It's the engine of the play. The director has to perceive how the arguments are developed and repeated, and mainly how the author has varied them in order not to be repetitious.

Argument can take many shapes. George Bernard Shaw had a particular social philosophy in mind, but each of his characters represents either concordant or opposing positions. In a Shaw play you get to think that everyone's point is valid. What stimulates the audience is listening to so many differing viewpoints on a particular subject. By the end of the play the character who represents Shaw's view will have either the closing argument or the most effective.

Brecht uses argument for paradox and contrast to demonstrate situations that he believes can be altered by political action. *The Good Woman of Setzuan* argues whether or not it is possible to be good in world that is poor. The central character wants to exist as a good woman, but she reverts to having to survive as a ruthless businessman. The play also argues how can a person not be ensnared in the web of lies, deceit, and cheating neighbors when the gods, if they exist at all, have messed everything up for us?

Chekhov's characters argue continuously with each other and with themselves. Half the characters are slamming doors, running into the woods, crying, and chasing each other with weapons, and half of them are frozen into immobility as they debate their own worth and usefulness.

A very interesting argument is the first act of *Cat on a Hot Tin Roof*, which is basically a monologue for Maggie, who is trying to get attention from her husband, Brick, who says almost nothing. His silence and laconic reaction to her tirades are his way of arguing: He pretends not to hear her problems, witticisms, and attempts at flattery and seduction. They have no effect on him; he is totally passive and unresponsive to her as a person, a woman, and wife. It's a very powerful way of arguing with Maggie, who is itching for a fight so that she can get everything out into the open. But Brick doesn't want anything out in the open. He wants to hurt her, and the best way that he can think of is to kill her with silence. The core of their argument is that she is fighting to keep him, and he wants her to go away.

Turning Points.   Embedded within the structure are moments in which the character or characters are offered certain opportunities that will change their circumstances. The change can be large or small, for better or worse. But the character either by accepting or rejecting the opportunity creates a turning point in the action. After the point is turned the situation changes. The character has either won or lost something. In the structure of Greek tragedy the protagonist was sometimes offered a way out. "Don't pursue this course any more! Turn back!" But the character, being noble and capable of great suffering, did not take the easy way out. He did not run away. He stayed and confronted his fate.

Romeo does not want to kill Tybalt but is provoked into it. In a life full of turning points this event changes Romeo's life irrevocably. A turning point always creates a chemical reaction when it's tossed into the plot. In a way, plot wouldn't exist without turning points, which give it its verve and mutability.

An Ibsen play is built upon one turning point after the other. No major character ever seems to finish a scene without one. In each scene a character is offered a choice of action or makes one independently. A turning point always happens as a result, but one of two things takes place. The character is aware that there has been a consequence for that choice and tries to move the action accordingly, or the character is unaware that there has been a turning point, and when unexpected complications transpire he or she suddenly tries to alter them. Ibsen usually prefers the latter because it's more interesting for the audience to see the characters fall into a hole and try to work themselves out. For example, in *A Doll's House* a turning point in Nora's life occurs when she tries to help her friend, Mrs. Elvsted, get a job in her husband's bank. Nora is trying to do a good turn. She's also showing off how much influence she has with her husband, who is about to become very important. But after Krogstadt, the man to whom she owes money and whose job is threatened by Mrs. Elvsted, hears of Nora's attempt, he pressures Nora with blackmail. If Nora had never put Mrs. Elvsted in Krogstadt's way, causing this particular turning point, the play would never happen. Hence, the turning point is an important mechanism of structure without which the plot can't develop or twist.

A play can have many turning points, some of which are so delicate and understated that they are barely perceptible. Toward the end of Chekhov's *The Cherry Orchard*, Lyubov is about to leave with her family. She is trying to get her adopted daughter, Varya, married to Lopahin, the man who bought her property.

Lyubov: You are well aware, Yermolay Alexeyevitch, I dreamed of marrying her to you, and everything seemed to show that you would get married. She loves you—she suits you. And I don't know—I don't know why it is you seem, as it were, to avoid each other. I can't understand it.

Lopahin: I don't understand it, myself, I confess. If there's still time, I'm ready now. Let's settle it straight off, and go ahead; but without you I feel I shan't make her an offer.

Lyubov: That's excellent. Why, a single moment's all that's necessary. I'll call her at once.
             (*A few moments later Lopahin and Varya are alone.*)

Varya: (*looking awhile over the things*): It is strange, I can't find it anywhere.

Lopahin: What are you looking for?

Varya: I packed it myself, and I can't remember (*a pause*).

Lopahin: Where are you going now, Varvara Mihailovna?

Varya: I? To the Ragulins. I have arranged to go to them to look after the house—as a housekeeper.

Lopahin: That's in Yashnovo? It'll be seventy miles away (*a pause*). So this is the end of life in this house!

Varya: (looking among the things):   Where is it? Perhaps I put it in the trunk. Yes, life in this house is over—there will be no more of it.

Lopahin:	And I'm just off to Kharkov—by this next train. I've a lot of business there. I'm leaving Epihodov here, and I've taken him on.
Varya:	Really!
Lopahin:	This time last year we had snow already, if you remember; but now it's so fine and sunny. Though it's cold, to be sure—three degrees of frost.
Varya:	I haven't looked (*a pause*). And besides, our thermometer's broken (*a pause*).
	(*Voice at the door from the yard calls Lopahin.*)
Lopahin:	This minute!
	(*He leaves quickly, and Varya, sitting on the floor and laying her head on a bag full of clothes, sobs quietly.*)

Lopahin has not taken the opportunity that he said he wanted. The desired turning point of the scene would have been his asking, "Will you marry me?" But never getting to it, he leaves Varya high and dry, lost with unfulfilled expectations. The turning point in this scene in when she says, "The thermometer is broken" and then the pause. Talk of the weather turns the conversation from being personal to being impersonal and distant. The turning point is a recognition of sorts for Varya. She sees that Lopahin will never propose. All her chances for marriage are gone: "The thermometer is broken, my heart is broken, our relationship is broken."

Aristotelian Elements.   What is the difference between naturalism and realism? Is Chekhov realism or the other way around? Gorki's *The Lower Depths* seems to be similar to a Chekhov play, but it's more socially attuned. Does that make the play naturalism? Questions like these would be simply and succinctly posed by my directing teacher, Larry Carra. "In a major Chekhov play and Gorki's *The Lower Depths* what is the dominant Aristotelian element?" All of us in his class ran to our copy of *Poetics* and discovered the six elements that our teacher was talking about: plot, character, thought, language, spectacle, and song.

We concluded that the dominant element in a Chekhov play was character. Yes, there were plot, language, and so forth, but the plays seemed to be studies in character behavior. As a matter of fact, we knew that Chekhov had been criticized by his peers for a lack of ide-

ology. He never proffered a political system in his plays or dramatized a need for social change. This kind of play, the one that emphasizes character, is naturalism.

A play like Gorki's *The Lower Depths*, which also has plot and character, does, however, emphasize thought or idea: It is a polemic, a
vision of political action for the underclass. This kind of play is realism.

The plays of George Bernard Shaw definitely would be called
realism because he was always expounding a new world order and
the possibility of the perfectibility of humankind.

It became very fashionable to dispute all this. "You're putting
labels on things, reducing art to the lowest common denominator by
these old-fashioned *isms*. Why are you referring to something as
obsolete as Aristotle, who was talking about tragedy and who was
wrong half the time?" And by the late sixties playwrights wanted to
weave naturalism, realism, song and dance, and everything else into
their plays. There was a conscious attempt to break down the old
conventions of structure. A play couldn't be pigeon-holed by any *ism*.

But there are good reasons to examine a play for its emphasis of
the Aristotelian elements. If you take a play apart to see how it was
put together, you will find plot, character, thought, language, spectacle, or song used in its construction as the steel beams upon which
everything else is placed.

Let's interpret these elements as they exist today.

1. Plot.   This also means *story* in this case. Plot can be simple or
complex. Samuel Beckett doesn't tell much of a story. We can't say that
Endgame or *Waiting for Godot* have been structured on their story. Murder mysteries and commercial comedies depend on story. *Dracula*,
which was adapted from the novel, is a great story. The play has some
interesting characters and some rather dull ones, but it's safe to say
that story and plot are the dominant elements in this play's structure.

2. Character.   Chekhov, as a doctor, saw characters from a clinical
point of view. He sliced all their virtues and faults down the middle
and showed them to us under his microscope. His plays emphasize
this element, a study in human behavior. The structure of his plays is
seemingly structureless: They give the appearance of looseness, life
coming in and out, spontaneity, awkwardness, and everything that

happens being random and absurd. But the plays are intensely structured as much as a poem is. The characters—often messy, wild, incoherent, overemotional—are actually carefully shaped and developed
and dominate the play they are in.

3. Thought.   This also means *idea*, or *theme*, or *message*. When this
is the dominant element, the play has something on its mind and
wants you to leave the theatre knowing what it is. Brecht labeled his
theatrical technique as "epic theatre." He used engrossing stories,
exotic songs, innovative stagecraft, and brilliant characters to present
a worldview of what is wrong with the human condition and how it
should be corrected. He wanted the audience to leave the theatre
thinking about the ideas that he was dramatizing. So did George
Bernard Shaw and Ibsen. A play of ideas, however, does not necessarily emphasize political action or social problems. Pirandello takes
the idea of illusion versus reality and builds both these ideas as the
basis of most of his plays.

4. Language.   All good plays are built on language. There is language as words, language as movement or mime, and the language of
silence. If you say that the dominant element of a play is language,
that suggests that the play is all rhetoric and fancy talk for the sake of
itself. However, it's fair to say that works of heightened poetry, such
as Shakespeare, or jewel-like minimalism, such as Samuel Beckett,
emphasize language. Simile, metaphor, allusion, wit, repartee, and
jokes are essential ingredients that give a Beckett play its distinction
and color. People argue over the meaning of a Beckett play—what
are its mystical or metaphysical or existential significances, that sort
of thing. I think Beckett saw life as something that we must endure
and get on with even though it is almost impossibly difficult at times.
And what gets us through is language because all our despair and
hope are in what we say. Even if we don't do anything, or can't do
anything, just saying it takes us halfway home. If the existentialists
declared, "You are what you do," I think that Beckett is saying, "You
are what you're saying you're going to do."

5. Spectacle.   This is when the audience goes out humming the
scenery. Spectacle has often replaced content in the musical

theatre. The audience is giving more applause to the scene changes than to the musical number. The changes of decor, new costumes, and spectacular lighting effects are built into the evening as carefully as an Ibsen plot or a Chekhov character. However, spectacle can place events on a larger-than-life canvas and give a production style and a sense of event. Spectacle can create the effect of humanity being caught up by large-scale events that it can either control or be dictated by. Spectacle pitches the drama out of the ordinary and attempts to place its characters in the middle of a great adventure.

6. Song.   There is tremendous variety in the way songs can be used in plays. Even Brecht, who used songs regularly, always had a different use for them within the same play. In *The Good Woman*, for instance, the water-seller sings a song to tell the audience what he does. Another song in the same play reveals the psychological state of the heroine, and another seems to confront the audience about the tedium of laboring in a tobacco factory.

If opera is about singing, the musical theatre is about the song. Every composer looks at a potential project and asks, "Does it sing?" The two things about the song in a musical that the director must observe are (a) where it's placed in the overall structure and (b) how the song is structured. In a musical the book is a vehicle for the songs. It is structured so that each song happens out of necessity and quite naturally. It must advance the story. The song itself can be structured in many ways: as a ballad, a patter song, a duet, a soliloquy, a dance, a mood piece, and so forth. Fundamentally a song can:

- Express the tone of the show.
- Tell us what the characters want.
- Expose secrets about the characters' inner lives.
- Celebrate an occasion or event within the action.
- Step out of the action and make a particular comment.

A song is a lyric moment, that is, it can depict intense feelings of love, passion, dreams, or other heightened emotions in ways that mere dialogue can't.

CHECKLIST

As you prepare, and even as you are in rehearsal, you will want to constantly go over the following:

1. Is my initial response to the play still there? Keep your gut reaction to the play intact. It's what first stimulated you and drew you into the material. It's what you want to share with the audience. When you're lost during production, it's there for you to fall back on because it's where all your instincts were born.

2. Do I know what the author is getting at? Keep at "What's this play about?" until you are satisfied that you have answered the question and your answer is on the stage. You don't have to be rigid in your thinking. You can be open to exploring all kinds of ideas. But you have to settle on something before production begins. The idea of rehearsal is to evolve your thinking, not to abandon it completely for something else.

3. Are all the characters clear in my mind? Examine the function of the characters and their purpose in the play. You will have some ideas that will be shaped and metamorphosed as you collaborate with the actors. Make sure that everyone's work reflects the intention of the play.

4. Is the play alive? Keep plugging away to get more and more of the play to "happen" onstage using internal events, external events, recognitions, and reversals.

5. How well do I know this play? Dig into the structure of the play by examining it endlessly for length, exposition, mystery, argument, turning points, and the Aristotelian elements of plot, character, thought, language, spectacle, and song.

6. Am I on firm ground? As you become aware of the play's structure you will see how it reflects its content and meaning. As you begin to make choices for production, you will know what the right ones are because you will know what the play is, what it demands, and what will reveal it.

CHAPTER FIVE

LANGUAGE

The heart of a play is its use of language. Each play's music comes from how the characters use words. Words externalize the intention of the text. The characters use words to directly state what they are thinking, feeling, and wanting, or they use words to cover emotions, avoid exposure, and keep their inner life covert. Words can mirror the darkest recesses of a character, or they can work to mask truth and reality.

The problem with many student-directed productions is their disuse—or, I should say, nonuse—of words. People who have control over directors, such as teachers or producers, are often more interested in how the concept will look than in how the content will sound. "What's your visual metaphor going to be? What new hook do you have on the material? Are we going to get something innovative and exciting from you?" Young directors respond in kind: "Yes, I'm going to have a trampoline out the door, so that when Nora leaves at the end of *A Doll's House*, she will literally leap into the twenty-first century!" (Don't laugh. This was actually done somewhere.) You may ask, "What about all those words, all that talk the characters do? What are you going to do with that?" Ignore it. Not out of deliberate intention, but out of a complete unawareness that it exists. Or if it does exist, it's something to wade through or cut until the next visual idea. This is not to discount the visual aspect of the theatre but rather to stress the increasingly neglected area of text and language.

Directors go into rehearsal unaware that the language of the play has been labored over and deliberately selected by the author, unaware that each character speaks in a specific way, with specific rhythms, and unaware that the audience can derive enormous pleasure from listening to language of the play if it's being well spoken. When cornered into explaining their nonuse of language, directors invariably blame the actors. "That's their lack of training. They should know how to do this." But directors who hide behind this excuse are like young film directors who hide behind the camera, afraid to talk to their actors. However, all is not dire. Once in awhile a director, when asked why he chose a particular play, will say, "Because I loved its use of language."

Look upon the words, idioms, rhythms, dialect, images, and manner of speech as the ways that the author has painted each character. Speech reveals the character's temperament, volatility, class, status, ego, and desires, as well as what the character is pursuing and to what degree. It is also writing style, which delineates one playwright from another. You cannot direct a Joe Orton play like one by Neil Simon. The language in an Orton play is honed into switchblade knives. The characters are ruthless and half insane. They are amoral and verge on cartoons. They talk in aphorisms, puns, and jokes and verbalize their most outrageous desires. Simon's language is middle-class America, usually second-generation Jewish, funny, and a little closer to the reality of everyday life. Orton's characters live by their wits and will survive at any cost. Simon's live by their sentimentality, angst, and need to be liked.

Examine a play by Tennessee Williams and by Arthur Miller. Look at a play by Eugene O'Neill and one by David Mamet, and you're listening to completely different music. A director has to have a good ear. He or she has to hear the author's music. And if you're not born with perfect pitch, you must work many years to acquire it, if you are going to direct.

Note: One of the reasons why language is neglected in productions is because the director has no time to deal with it. He or she never really gets to work with actors until production time. By then there are so many demands that taking time out to sit with the actors and go over the details and nuances of the text seems unthinkable. But the point is that you have to. When you get to staging the play, making its language work will be one of your key jobs. A way of preparing yourself for skills in this area is to practice. Start an old-fashioned play-reading group whose members sit down together and read a play a week. Make an arrangement with some actors to work on text as discussed over the next several pages.

LYRICAL LANGUAGE

Shakespeare's *Twelfth Night* is a perfect example of how an author paints with language. The forlorn Duke Orsino, who lives on unrequited love, is bursting with metaphor and with florid poetry. He is both absurd and pitiful. Viola's language works on two levels because she herself is on two levels: as a woman and as a woman pretending to be a man. Her language is alternately simple, direct, and spare on the one hand and full of poetical double meaning on the other. The clowns, Sir Toby and Sir Andrew, are like middle-aged college fraternity boys. They have a code language all their own, full of jests and witticisms that only they understand. Malvolio is etched in the language he uses. His manner of speech is pretentious, condescending, full of self-love, and always ridiculous. The language in the play goes from verse to prose. What's the difference? Do only the upper classes in the play speak in poetic language? Are Toby and the clowns lower class or everyday people because they speak in prose? No, because many of the clowns in the play are upper class themselves.

The romantic aspect of the play is written in verse. In musicals the characters can express themselves in song only because ordinary speech doesn't express the heightened emotion being felt at the time. The need to sing is the same as the need to speak in verse. It's just another kind of lyric moment. Not that the actor has to sing the poetry. But there has to be an overflow of feeling and a need to express it that goes beyond the way you and I talk to each other.

Exploring the Opening of *Twelfth Night*

Enter Orsino (Duke of Illyria), Curio and other Lords (and musicians).

Duke: If music be the food of love, play on:
Give me excess of it, that, surfeiting,
The appetite may sicken, and so die.
That strain again! It had a dying fall;
O, it came o'er my ear like the sweet sound
That breathes upon a bank of violets,

Stealing and giving odor! Enough, no more!
'Tis not so sweet now as it was before.
O spirit of love, how quick and fresh art thou,
That, notwithstanding thy capacity
Receiveth as the sea, naught enters there,
Of what validity and pitch soe'er,
but falls into abatement and low price
Even in a minute! So full of shapes is fancy
That it alone is high fantastical.

Image Exercise

At this point work with an actor to develop your sense of language in order to see how language is both challenging and illuminating.

Rather than try to scan the stresses and beats of iambic pentameter, it might be more effective to work to make sense of the images in the speech.

music, food of love

play on

excess

appetite, sicken, die

strain again

sweet smells and sweet sounds

dying fall

These are some of the images in just the first five lines of the speech. They are concrete and identifiable.

"If music be the food of love, play on" is a command or an invocation. It is one thought said by a man whose brain is in a love fever.

Have the actor close his eyes and say just these words. What do these images evoke? These key words are all very open sounding: *music, food, love, play on*. Orsino is shamelessly in love. He opens the play confessing his passions to the world. As a matter of fact, he wants "excess of it" so that "surfeiting / The appetite may sicken, and so die." He'd like to gorge himself on music until he desires it no longer. He feels the same way about love.

Try to work with the actor until the feeling is free and open, not pulled in the back of the throat or reticent. Perhaps the actor will relate to an unrequited love that he has experienced or a longing that he wishes were satiated.

Make sure that:

1. The actor does not fragment the lines by mistiming his breath. The breath has to be sufficient to encompass the sense of the whole line, not just parts of the line.
2. Breath is not exhaled before the actor says the lines, leaving the actor with not enough oxygen to complete the thoughts.
3. The ends of sentences are reached with clarity. This means that there is enough breath to convey the entire thought. Acting has to be on the breath. The common misconception is that the actor exhales to relax before saying the line. As a result, however, there is no breath left to finish the line. This is why the ends of sentences are always dropped and so many unnecessary pauses have to take place while air is gulped in.

The images in the first five lines are very concrete and sensual: love, hearing, tasting, and smelling. Then the speech becomes very abstract: The duke cuts off his desires and deliberately begins to intellectualize the situation. It's as if the character has decided to stop feeling about love and start thinking about it instead. At this point the lines are quite long:

> O spirit of love, how quick and fresh art thou,
> That, notwithstanding thy capacity
> Receiveth as the sea, naught enters there
> Of what validity and pitch soe'er,
> But falls into abatement and low price
> Even in a minute.

Verb Exercise

After working on all the images of the speech, try having the actor say only the verbs. In other words, the actor goes through the speech in his own mind but says only the following out loud.

be

play on

give me

surfeiting

sicken

die

had

came

breathes

stealing

giving

'tis not

was

art thou

receiveth

enters

falls

is

is

Try this several times and slowly have the actor add on whatever words in the speech that he feels are necessary. Build on this until the entire speech is finally spoken audibly. By this time the images will be clearer and each word needed, each word earned.

This does not mean that each word is stressed or overenunciated. It means that the actor is connected to the language in a way that makes personal or imaginative sense.

The Dialect Exercise

Ask the actor to do the speech using a dialect such as a southern gentleman, Italian noble, or Irish romantic. Suddenly the phrasing of the lines, the timing of breath, and overall sense will become vividly alive. It's as though the actor's inner ear opens, and he can hear exactly how to land on each word and what effect each word is having. As he hears himself doing the speech his instincts lead him to deliver it in a very colorful and humorous way.

Repeat the speech and see if you and the actor can find a bridge between what was done with the dialect and what needs to be done with whatever interpretation you are working on.

Real-Life Exercise

After the speech seems to flow naturally from the actor, there's a good chance that a character is beginning to emerge and a story is being told. The character is mainly constructed on what he or she says and on the manner in which it is being said. The actor and director might want to relate to Orsino as something more than an Elizabethan duke who lived in a never-never land a long time ago. Who is Orsino today? Do we know any guys like this? Who talks like this? Certainly no one on the planet today.

But wait.

There are people who always have to be in love. They are often melancholy and fickle. They are in love with only the unattainable. They love talking metaphorically, almost poetically, about their feelings. Sometimes we listen to them and don't quite know what they are talking about. If we open our ears, we've heard Orsinos before: relatives, friends, someone we've had a relationship with, and so forth.

Ask the actor to do a real-life study of someone who has a few of Orsino's qualities. After the portrayal, suggest that he try Orsino's speech as that person. See if any of Orsino travels to the real-life study or the real-life study to Orsino.

CHARACTER RHYTHM

How a character uses words, images, and verbal argument and, in general, deals with language creates both a speaking rhythm and an inner rhythm. The character has been scored like an instrument in an orchestra to sound a certain way and to accompany or contrast the various other parts in the play.

In John Guare's *The House of Blue Leaves*, the central character, Artie Shaughnessy, is a dreamer. He's slow to take action, slow to make major decisions, slow to leave his mentally ill wife. He's a nice guy who doesn't want to hurt anyone, but he is burning up with ambition to change his life.

On the other hand we have Bunny Flingus, who is the workhorse of the play. She's a fast-talking, self-assertive dynamo who is going to whirl Artie and herself out of Queens, New York, and into Hollywood. She pushes all the action forward and tries whenever she can to be the catalyst to any situation that is to her advantage. She's a very funny character because her use of language is often pretentious and overdone. She is, in many ways, the female equivalent of Malvolio. She's had "greatness thrust upon her" and is on her way! Hers is a very particular music: rhythmical, quick, and energetic but possessed with genuine, if slightly absurd, lyricism.

She makes her first entrance shortly after the start of the first act. It's the day that the pope is to visit New York for the first time. She knocks on the door of her boyfriend, Artie Shaughnessy, a zookeeper, who is a would-be songwriter and who is married.

Artie is sleeping, he hears a key in the door, gets out of his bed, undoes the bolts on the door, and jumps back into his sleeping bag on his bed. Bunny enters.

Bunny: You know what your trouble is? You got no sense of history. You know that? Are you aware of that? Lock yourself up against history, get drowned in the whole tide of human events. Sleep it away in your bed. Your bag. Zip yourself in, Artie. The greatest tide in the history of the world is coming in today, so don't get your feet wet.

Artie: It's quarter to five in the morning, Bunny—

Bunny: Lucky for you I got a sense of history. (*She picks up the newspaper on the floor.*) You finish last night's? Oooo, it's freezing out there. Breath's coming out of everybody's mouth like a balloon in a cartoon.

(*She rips the paper into long shreds and stuffs it down into the plastic booties she wears.*)

People have been up for hours. Queens Boulevard—lined for blocks already! Cripples laid out in the streets in stretchers with ear muffs on over their bandages. Nuns—you never seen so many nuns in your life! Ordinary people like you and me in from New Jersey and Connecticut and there's a lady even drove in from Ohio — Ohio! — just for today! She drove four of the most crippled people in Toledo. They're stretched out in the gutter waiting for the sun to come out so they can start snapping pictures. I haven't seen so many people, Artie, so excited since the premiere of *Cleopatra*. It's that big. Breathe! There's miracles in the air!

Artie: It's soot, Bunny. Polluted air.

Bunny: And when he passes by in his limousine, I'll call out, "Your Holiness, marry us — the hell with peace to the world — bring peace to us." And he won't hear me because bands will be playing and the whole city yelling, but he'll see me because I been eyed by the best of them, and he'll nod and I'll grab your hand and say, "Marry us, Pope," and he'll wave his holy hand and all the emeralds and rubies on his fingers will send Yes beams. In a way today is my wedding day. I should have something white at my throat! Our whole life is beginning — my life — our life — and we'll be married and go out to California. . . .

Bunny gives inspiration and life to Artie because she doubts nothing and has complete faith in her belief, which is Artie's talent. She galvanizes the play.

Exercise: Experiment with the Actress in the Following Ways

1. Do the verb exercise.
2. Try the speech in a strong New York accent.
3. Do the speech without an accent.
4. Imagine that Bunny is praying on her knees or sitting in a church pew. She closes her eyes and experiences the pope, her dreams, California.
5. Do the speech as a comedian at a standup club entertaining the audience.
6. Say the speech on one breath. On two breaths. On three. Reduce the intake of oxygen in order to keep the speech from fragmenting.

7. Add physicality. Perhaps the actress is reminded of a certain animal while playing Bunny. Have her transform into that animal. Add the sounds that that animal would make. Does this rhythm match your conception of the role? Add some of Bunny's lines to the animal.

8. The actress plays Bunny again, this time sustaining the inner rhythm or dynamic of the animal, and adds the text.

REVEALING A CHARACTER'S INNER CONFLICTS

A character can articulate great changes of mood, feeling, and opinion in a single speech. The volatility of a character can be expressed in what he or she says, how it's said, and what is not being said. Nina's speech toward the end of *The Sea Gull* is a good example.

Nina: Why do you say you kiss the ground I walk on? I ought to be killed. (*bends over desk*) I'm so tired. If I could rest . . . rest. I'm a sea gull. No, that's not it. I'm an actress. Well, no matter . . . (*hears Arkadina and Trigorin laughing in the dining room, listens, runs to the door on the left, and peeps through the keyhole*) And he's here, too. (*goes to Trepleff*) Well, no matter. He didn't believe in the theatre, all my dreams he'd laugh at, and little by little I quit believing in it myself, and lost heart. And there was the strain of love, jealousy, constant anxiety about my little baby. I got to be small and trashy, and played without thinking. I didn't know what to do with my hands, couldn't stand properly on the stage, couldn't control my voice. You can't imagine the feeling when you are acting and know it's dull. I'm a sea gull. No, that's not it. Do you remember, you shot a sea gull? A man comes by chance, sees it, and out of nothing else to do destroys it. That's not it . . . (*puts her hand to her forehead*) What was I . . . I was talking about the stage. Now I'm not like that. I'm a real actress, I act with delight, with rapture, I'm drunk when I'm on stage, and feel that I am beautiful. And now, ever since I've been here, I've kept walking about, kept walking and thinking, thinking and believing my soul grows stronger every day. Now I know, I understand, Kostya, that in our work . . . acting or writing . . . what matters is not fame, not glory, not what I used to dream about, it's how to endure, to bear my cross, and have faith. I have faith and it all doesn't hurt me so much, and when I think of my calling I'm not afraid of life . . .

Whereas Bunny has enormous belief in herself, Nina is struggling to find some. The language used in Nina's speech is simple, direct, yet metaphorical as she compares herself with a sea gull.

Observe:

How she flip-flops from identifying who she is: a sea gull, something that can be shot down and destroyed, or an actress, an artist who can live creatively.

How she delves into a painful past and compares herself again with a helpless sea gull, but then refutes this.

How she attributes Trepleff killing a sea gull to being bored but instantly realizes that there was more to it than that.

How she admits now that she is a real actress. How she can live separated from Trigorin.

Moreover, it's important to note that a well-written speech like this invariably:

- Has a purpose. There is a dramatic purpose. The placement of the speech in the text is designed as part of the play's structure. The speech can't go any other place in the play, and it cannot be cut from it. It's vital to the meaning of the play. There is also a character purpose for the speech. The character wants something. The speech is a means of getting it. Without a purpose, the character has no need to say the speech.
- Has an event within it. Speeches aren't meditations or musings. As you can see, something very important happens onstage toward the end of Nina's speech. She recognizes who she is and what she must do with her life.

- Results in the action of the play moving forward. The speech is an event that moves the story forward. Nina has grown, has her art, and is not afraid of life anymore. It's a catharsis for her. Ironically, Trepleff recognizes that he is not loved, that he cannot endure, and a few moments later takes his own life. He hasn't her faith.

REPARTEE AND INTERPLAY OF DIALOGUE

Repartee is the witty and quick conversation that goes on between the characters. It's a hallmark of comedy, but it exists in "serious" drama as well. It is the verbal give-and-take between characters. The actors have to be very finely tuned to each other in terms of listening and responding. They have to be fully concentrated and focused. Repartee is like two acrobats working together: One false move, and the act has fallen into the net.

1. Cues have to be picked up in a timely fashion. The actor receiving the ball can't practice his backstroke and expect to hit the ball back if he wants to stay in the game. The scene will fall flat if one actor is taking too much time to "act" or think before speaking.
2. The lines have to be delivered precisely, as written. There can be no extraneous words ad-libbed, no "ahs" or "umms."
3. Pauses are orchestrated, not randomly sprinkled all over the text. They cannot be used as a crutch or actor's tick or for meaningful "effect."
4. The ends of lines cannot be dropped. A dropped line is a dropped action. It lets all the steam out of the moment and disables the other actors from coming in correctly.

Think of repartee as music wherein each instrument has to come in for its answer or response precisely and in meter.

Example

Let's take a look at the famous scene between Beatrice and Benedick in *Much Ado about Nothing,* where they confess their love for each other. A disturbing incident has just taken place: Hero, Beatrice's cousin, has just been accused of unfaithfulness by Claudio, the man Hero was about to marry. Claudio is Benedick's best friend. Beatrice is outraged at what happened and is crying bitterly as Benedick approaches.

The relationship between Beatrice and Benedick up until now has been combative and abrasive as each tries to top the other in rudeness and insults. They have been like oil and water. Yet they have had one thing in common: language. They both adore puns, verbal put-downs, and using their wits to assault one another. To a large extent, they are a match made in heaven. In the meantime, Beatrice and Benedick have been duped into thinking that each of them has fallen in love with the other. But right now, the business at hand is what Claudio has done to Hero.

Benedick: Lady Beatrice, have you wept all this   1
while?

Beatrice: Yes, and I will weep a while longer.   2

Benedick: I will not desire that.   3

Beatrice: You have no reason; I do it freely.   4

Benedick: Surely, I do believe your fair cousin   5
is wronged.

Beatrice: Ah, how much might the man deserve   6
of me that would right her!

Benedick: Is there any way to show such friendship?   7

Beatrice: A very even way, but no such friend.   8

Benedick: May a man do it?   9

Beatrice: It is a man's office, but not yours.   10

Benedick: I do love nothing in the world so well as   11
you; is not that strange?

Beatrice: As strange as the thing I know not.   12
It were as possible for me to say I   13
loved nothing so well as you;
but believe me not; and yet I lie not;   14
confess nothing, nor I deny nothing. I am   15
sorry for my cousin.

Benedick: By my sword, Beatrice, thou lovest me.   16

Beatrice: Do not swear and eat it.   17

Benedick: I will swear by it that you love me; and   18
          I will make him eat it that says I love
          you not.
Beatrice: Will you eat your word?   19
Benedick: With no sauce that can be devised to it.   20
          I protest I love thee.
Beatrice: Why then, God forgive me!   21
Benedick: For what offense, sweet Beatrice?   22
Beatrice: You have stayed me in a happy hour: 23
          I was about to protest I loved you.   24
Benedick: And do it with all thy heart.   25
Beatrice: I love you with so much of my heart that   26
          none is left to protest.
Benedick: Come, bid me do anything for thee.   27
Beatrice: Kill Claudio.   28

Examine the following:

Repeats.   It is sometimes useful for the actor to pick up the rhythm
or emphasis of the preceding line or word if it's repeated.

> (Line 1) have you wept all this while?
> (Line 2) I will weep a while longer. . . .

Argument.   Statements opposing each other have to be cleanly laid
out.

> (Line 3) I will not desire that.
> (Line 4) You have no reason; I do it freely.

Contrast.   The language expresses two opposing points, each of
which must be clearly stated: wrong and right.

> (Line 5) Surely, I do believe your fair cousin is wronged.
> (Line 6) Ah, how much might the man deserve of me that
> would right her!

Repeats again:

> (Line 7)   . . . any way to show such friendship?
> (Line 8)   . . . very even way, but no such friend.

> (Line 9) May a man do it?
> (Line 10) It is a man's office. . . .
> (Line 11) . . . is not that strange?
> (Line 12) As strange as the thing I know not.

Volatility.   The character is ambivalent about what he or she means. Or she wants to say something but is not sure that she should say it. She hides behind language, using it as a denial, but in denial she expresses everything.

> (Lines 13–15) It were as possible for me to say I loved noth-
> ing so well as you; but believe me not; and yet I lie not; I
> confess nothing, nor I deny nothing. I am sorry for my
> cousin.

Jokes.   At the moment of passionate confession, these characters make jokes with one another. Of course, Beatrice jokes as a way of protecting herself because she's not quite sure of the depth of Benedick's feelings. These jokes are subtle but must be dealt with technically. That is, the repeats must be in rhythm, and the ends of the lines cannot be dropped. For example, if Beatrice drops the last word in "Will you eat your word?" Benedick's witticism, "With no sauce that can be devised to it," will make no sense.

> (Line 16) By my sword, Beatrice, thou lovest me.
> (Line 17) Do not swear and eat it.
> (Line 18) I will swear by it that you love me; and I will make
> him eat it that says I love you not.
> (Line 19) Will you eat your word?
> (Line 20) With no sauce that can be devised to it.

Rhythmic Structure.   Words and ideas weave in and out of each other to create a music of their own.

> (Line 20) . . . I protest I love thee.
> (Line 21) . . . God forgive me!
> (Line 22) For what offense. . . .
> (Lines 23–24) . . . I was about to protest I loved you.
> (Line 25) And do it with all thy heart.
> (Line 26) I love you . . . my heart . . . none left to protest.

Comic Surprise.   There is a sudden turn in the dialogue that shifts the action of the play.

> (Line 27) Come, bid me do anything for thee.
> (Line 28) Kill Claudio.

Timing.   The laugh that Beatrice gets on "Kill Claudio" depends on her timing. One actress took almost a minute before she said the line. Benedick asked her to bid him do anything, and she looked at him and practically did a "take" to the audience and let the anticipation of what she would answer build in titters until she knew she had the audience right where she wanted it and delivered the line. But everyone's timing is different, and another actress couldn't get away with this. Timing is very individual, and the director needs to feel this out with the actors. The real key to timing is that when working out the "Kill Claudio" moment the character's intentions must be held on to. This is a dream for her. Beatrice now has a man she loves who will give her the one thing she wants: revenge!

QUESTIONS TO ASK OF YOURSELF

Is the language of the text clear? The actors and writers rely on the director as the objective ear of the play. The trap is that you have heard the text so many times that you think it's being articulated when it's not. As the production moves from rehearsal room to its playing space, you have to make sure that the actors' "size" is increased accordingly. Too many actors believe that the so-called intimacy they found in rehearsals will be lost if the audience hears them. They pull everything down to a whisper. Have the actor play out his or her text fully. You will find that the fuller the language, the fuller the feeling.

Are the ends of sentences being dropped and therefore not heard? When the actor's breathing is mistimed every sentence ends in a downward inflection because there's no breath left for the end of the line. The context of the line is lost. Make doubly sure that the actor does not exhale before speaking. This is a misconception about relaxation. Actors exhale out of nervousness and leave nothing to say the line on. Acting, as many well-known stars have declared, is done on the breath.

Are the lines being read correctly? Many actors are phobic about being given a line reading and intimidate directors into not doing this. However, the director should not be bullied by this. If you feel that a word is not being colored or that a point is being missed, you can only help the actor, the production, and the audience by pointing it out. And again, you are the person sitting out front and can hear it better than anyone else.

Is the actor droning, that is, elongating vowels and diphthongs? Due either to inexperience, nervousness, or unawareness young actors tend to drone or drawl out their words in performance. They strike an even, unvarying vocal quality; and between the elongation of sounds and the amount of breath that it takes to say a single sentence the audience becomes impatient and bored. These elongated sounds stretch out the sentence, and all meaning is lost. "I want to go to the store" takes so long to say that the audience forgets the word *want* by the time the actor gets to *store*.

There has to be a difference between rehearsal rhythm and performance rhythm. In the rehearsal the actor is exploring, groping for lines, searching for meaning, squeezing out every drop of emotion. But by the time the performance comes around, the actor needs to have transcended all that and to have become the character whose timing, responses, and actions are different than her own.

Is the actor overadjusting to your notes? The director sometimes wishes that a note had never been given. That idea that you had about a phrasing for a certain part of a certain line is now being so overstressed, so overarticulated by the actor that it now seems lifeless and arbitrary. The actor has taken your note, agreed with it, and is punching it mercilessly. You have to ask the actor to, "Just feel it, don't stress it at all."

Some lines work best when "thrown away." This is tossing the line off in an unexpected and off-handed manner. The audience wants to say, "Did he say what I think he said? That's outrageous." The line is said almost as an aside to oneself or to the audience. It's a delicate balancing act between seeming very casual but being carefully phrased at the same time.

"Walking out of the joke" or important point is an effective technique. The actor knows he's got a funny line, says it to the other actor, and moves away. It's like dumping a load of mischief in someone's lap and leaving. The laugh comes not only from the joke itself, but also from the "take" by the actor who is responding to it.

Is the note that you gave the actor wrong? You had this fabulous idea about the reading of a line. You've told the actor. She tried it. You thought you liked it. As rehearsals go on, the actor not only has rhythms and timing of her own, but also she has evolved something special about Bunny. That piece of direction you gave her is like a monkey wrench in her path. It is now the wrong way to do that particular line. You tell the actor, but she likes it. She's come to love it like an article of clothing that is hopelessly out of style.

But the truth is that her performance is transcending your directions in the sense that she has metamorphosed into the character, and those earlier ideas of yours now seem grafted on like an unneeded appendage. You tell the actor to eliminate those earlier adjustments.

Directing is also taking away direction.

FREQUENTLY ASKED QUESTIONS

Q: I'm kind of gun shy about working with actors so technically. What can I do?

A: What do you mean by that?

Q: The image exercise, the verb exercise, dealing with breath, practically giving line readings at times. Shouldn't the actor be able to work more from his feelings so that the language will happen by itself?

A: The language will never happen by itself if it's not happening to begin with. There's nothing wrong with technique or being "technical." And don't forget: Those wonderful feelings of the actors that you extol can happen only by another kind of technique.

Q: Can you tell me more about real-life exercises?

A: You observe a person and bring your portrayal into class or rehearsal as an exercise. Then you see if you can incorporate the person into the role you are working on. You will never find one person who is your character. You may eventually end up with a composite of people you've observed. The main factor in all this is that the exercise helps you humanize your character if you see parts of him in others.

Q: Character rhythm is in the lines, as you've shown, but it's elsewhere, isn't it?

A: Yes. There is an inner rhythm that might be quite different than the rhythm of our speech. A person can think very fast and be almost frantic inside but have a slow speaking rhythm. Artie in *Blue Leaves* certainly thinks fast, is very alert and bright, and is burning up with ferocious energy. But he doesn't talk fast like Bunny.

Q: It's probably good that he doesn't so that you can get contrast between the two characters.

A: Yes, you don't want them playing each other's rhythm because there would be no musical contrast.

Q: Inner conflict can happen like Nina's in *The Sea Gull,* but it can also manifest itself in silence, can't it?

A: Yes. Silence is a language all its own. It's scored into many scripts by Beckett and Pinter. Much is said in the silence. It's up to the director and actors to fill it in. But silence should never be overused or sprinkled generously for theatrical effect. Nor should it permanently be the place where the actor usually forgets a particular line.

Q: I like the idea of repartee. How can I find out more about it?

A: Get recordings of old radio shows. Abbott and Costello's famous "Who's on First?" sketch is a classic example. Jack Benny, Lucille Ball, Burns and Allen all are on records and videos. Talk show hosts each night engage in endless repartee with their guests. When these shows are funniest is when the give-and-take of repartee is happening.

Q: It seems that the director has to be a great listener to hear every nuance and color and tone and intonation and phrase and rhythm of the text.

A: Start with being a *good* listener. Great comes later.

PART THREE

THE DIRECTOR AS COLLABORATOR

The nature of preparation.

Working with playwrights, producers, designers, and dramaturgs.

Techniques and strategies for working with actors from auditions to rehearsals and into the performance.

CHAPTER SIX

THE TEAM

When you direct, many people are dependent on you for answers—designers, stage managers, authors, choreographers, actors, producers, technicians, and so forth. They come to you because you are the final arbiter.

"Do you like this sofa?"

"What do you think of this color?"

"Can we move the wall two feet back?"

"Have you read my rewrite of the first act yet?"

"Do you think I'm shouting too much in the last scene?"

All of these people, who are quite expert in what they do, look to you to see if they are giving you what you want. It's a responsibility. The director is the leader of a team, but he should never forget that he is part of the team also. Theatre is the place where disparate egos come together and work off each other's creativity to make a successful show.

A collaboration, as rewarding as it often turns out to be, can be volatile, emotional, upsetting, and soul-searching, with people passionately disagreeing with each other. Or, a collaboration can be an absolute lovefest, where everyone is hugging and kissing and "darling"ing each other to death and where it's smooth sailing from the first day. The director is very instrumental in setting the tone and atmosphere of the workplace.

There was a famous director, who shall remain nameless, who thrived on making everyone around him miserable. He would scream, throw things, walk out, come back, calm down, and go into another tantrum. After the show was over, he would treat his victims as his best friends, having no regrets about how he behaved. He was not a malicious man or sadistic. He just had to have a lot of tension in the room to get himself energized. He couldn't take calm. It was anathema to him.

However, genuine debate and controversy can be very healthy if they're part of a nonadversarial and collegial partnership. If, for example, a designer and director argue, an alternative way that neither of them first thought of will usually evolve into a better solution in general.

The director wants everyone to do his or her best work, and he wants to get what he's after. In most cases, if all concerned know what the director wants, they will make every effort to give it to him. However, does the director know what he wants? If he does and articulates it to his team, magical things take place. As the leader of the team, the director has to come prepared to do his work and contribute to everyone else's.

PREPARATIONS

You are preparing yourself by doing the text work outlined in the preceding chapters: reading the play for your personal responses, examining its form and content, and locating what you think it's about. Although the essence of the theatrical collaboration is sharing, debating, and evolving ideas of what the play is about, everyone looks to the director as the guiding light. If the director carries any torch it's the one that is burning bright about his interpretation of the material.

Unless it's a new play and this is its first production, there are models for doing it. Many plays have a performance history that is easily researched and can be quite helpful. You certainly don't want to mimic a previous production, but you might want to know how others solved it. You might say, "They were all wrong about the way they did this play!" This reinforces your own theories. Or you might say, "Good grief, I never thought of that!" and find that although you don't want to do the same thing, something needs to be invented by you to achieve its equivalent.

And, of course, you've done research on the author, the world of the play, its social, historical, and political underpinnings, how art, music, and literature of the period are part of this play, and you have read commentaries and reviews of past productions.

It goes without saying that the director always enters the first day of rehearsal feeling as though he knows nothing. Tyrone Guthrie once told me that he starts every rehearsal "with my heart in my heels." I asked him when he began to feel confident. He said, "After the first few lines are read." No matter how well you are prepared you are always going to have a variation on what actors call "stage fright." It's scary going in and telling everyone what you think, what you think they should think, what to do, and how to do it. No matter how experienced you become, there's always doubt about yourself. But to doubt is positive. It really means that the director is saying, "Am I on the right road? If not, will I find the right road? Am I too locked in, or can I get out?" Always questioning yourself and your choices is not the worst thing that you can do.

And! A play is mysterious. It won't reveal its secrets to you all at once. But preparation will help your confidence that you have at least an approach to the play, and it will give everyone on the team confidence and respect for what you have to say.

Your preparation helps your collaboration with:

The Playwright

The basis of all theatrical collaborations is honesty. You have to be yourself. You have to articulate what you truly feel and believe. Sometimes you have to be painfully frank. There is no time for equivocation, trying to say things in a way that makes you seem like a nice guy and avoiding hurting the other person. A good collaboration cuts through all that. It demands that each person get to the heart of the matter clearly and as quickly as possible.

In today's theatre, directors from students to seasoned pros are directing new plays. Many more playwriting programs are attempting to produce the work of their writers and are calling on student directors to direct them. Those old barriers, such as, "We only do the classics here," are breaking down. The classics should be done, of course, for many reasons. Chiefly, these classics expand our skills and imagination. New writing, however, keeps the theatre alive. Many more regional theatres are committed to producing new plays. It seems that just about everyone is developing new material in readings, staged readings, workshops, and second stages, among a few examples.

You can be assigned a playwright's play by your department or by your theatre company or by a producer. This is a case where you have to do the play whether you like it or not and find yourself in a prearranged marriage. If you like the play, you're in luck. If you don't like the play, you can do one of two things: accept it on its own terms or try to help change it.

You can find a new play and love it so much that you are willing to do anything to get it produced, including shopping it around, taking it to meetings, convincing producers, and directing it for no money.

Once you get an assignment to direct a new play, you will often find that it needs changes and that the author is willing, ready, and able to do the work.

You may get in a situation, as well, where the author is intractable and won't change a line.

No matter what the situation is, you as the director have to keep one thing in mind: It is not your play! It is the writer's play. You cannot take it over and make it your thing. In films the director can do this because the screenwriter has sold the material outright and is no longer able to control it. After the studio has bought it, many other writers may be brought in to rewrite it. In the theatre, the writer has licensed the play to the producer and keeps artistic control over it.

You are the playwright's guide through the labyrinth of decisions, changes, and results that happen in production. And no matter what you think of the play, you are the author's advocate on the production. The director/playwright collaboration begins with:

1. Asking Pertinent Questions.   Start with, "Why did you write this play? What did it come out of?" From there go to specifics. "Why is she in this scene? Why does he say this, when in the last scene he said that?" Anything that bothers you or, I should say, anything that provokes your curiosity, no matter how obvious it may seem, should be brought up. You'll be surprised how effective these questions are because the writer is really thinking, "I didn't make that clear. Maybe I can find a better way. I wrote the play so long ago I've forgotten what my impulses were."

2. Editing.   If the play is too long, and plays often are, you have to encourage editing. This is a delicate issue. The writer may consider every word golden and balk at any suggestion of cuts. The solution is to rock the boat a little by sending out a few feelers in that direction. "Do we really need this three-page speech? I mean, it's wonderfully clear halfway through, and then I think the point gets a little labored." A constructive solution is to say, "Let's read the play as is, and then we'll talk about it." You do owe it to the writer to hear the play as written before you begin to prod further for cuts. After the reading the author may see that she has to trim that speech down. Or, you may have been dead wrong, and the speech is dynamite and shouldn't be touched. The worse scenario is that the speech doesn't work, the writer doesn't see it, and you know it's got to be cut. Can you cut it without her approval? No way! What's the solution? I leave that in your lap as it has been left in mine on many occasions and can say only, "Where there's a will, there's a way."

After previews begin the audience will tell you immediately if that speech is as long as you think it is. Most authors will come around by then. If he doesn't, say this: "Let's try it tonight my way and see if it works better. If it doesn't we'll go back to your way."

A collaboration is a two-way street. The author will have things to say about your direction, sometimes very drastic things such as, "You've made the characters real, and I wanted them to be automatons," or "She's hopeless. I never wanted her in the first place. Fire her and get someone else." Keep the author informed every inch of the way to avoid getting notes on things that it's too late and too difficult to do anything about.

3. Help by Making Visual Suggestions.   Many writers write on the word. They hear how the play sounds but don't always see it in the most visually effective way. A director can be of enormous help by suggesting physical settings for some scenes—atmosphere, weather conditions, and staging ideas. "What if we played this scene outdoors in the rain instead of having them sit at the table again?" The director's suggestions in this area are usually appreciated by the writer because they open the play up to more variety and can trigger a more exciting way to do the scene.

After you're in production the collaboration somewhat alters:

1. You can keep the writer out or invite her in. As I suggested, it's best to have the writer come as often as possible, although watching actors develop their roles is tedious for the writer who would rather be there when you're running through the play. After both the writer and director see how the play is functioning on its feet, the real work begins between you. You have joint custody of what's on stage by this point and will find yourselves artistically intertwined until the play opens. This becomes the time when you really listen to each other.

2. Hopefully the author will see for himself what is weak and needs to be fixed. In my experience this happens most of the time. There are times, however, when you will work with an author who cannot see that anything is wrong, who will not or cannot change the writing. Or there are times when the rewrites are not good. Again, it's the writer's play. The evening will rise or fall on its merits. Make the performances and production as strong as possible, and as for the outcome of the play itself, let the critical chips fall where they may.

3. You can try out new material and keep that flow coming. If you are receiving rewrites that are making the play better, you must encourage the process. A new play is untried, and a spirit of freedom and experimentation should dominate your rehearsals. Try improvising with the author present, try any transposition of dialogue that you think might work, help rearrange scenes, do the play backward or standing on its head. That's what rehearsals are for.

4. Keep the writer focused on what points are to be made. Always remind the author what the play is about and how you are trying to achieve it. You want to keep your goals clear and your vision of the play articulated. I once did a play in which everyone wanted the ending changed—the producers, the backers, and people who came to previews. The author and I were on the verge of caving in, but I said, "We're rising or falling on that ending. Don't change it. It's what the play is

about." That convinced the author. Fortunately, I was right. Had I been wrong, I'd now be saying, "Never go with what you believe the play is about. Go for what you think the audience wants."

The Producer

In the commercial, regional, and academic theatres, the "powers above" require specific preparation from the director. Technically the producer has raised the money for the production. If it's a commercial venture, he wants to make sure of his investment. If it's a not-for-profit production, he doesn't want to lose money, either. He has financial control over the entire production and will often be quite assertive artistically.

Your understanding of the play is probed: what you think it's about. Your concept is asked for: how you see it on stage. As practicalities—such as budget, time factors, theatre space, the availability of personnel, special conditions—are laid out for you, your mettle as a director is being tested. No director ever completely gets what she wants. This cruel awakening starts in academia. The student director learns by being given very little and overcoming one obstacle after another: not enough time, not enough technical support, almost no budget, actors who are not ideal, and so forth. However, lack of resources should not mean a lack of directorial invention and ingenuity. The challenge is to become ever more inventive as everything that you thought you wanted seems to be taken from you.

The producer/director collaboration is the most difficult one. It's two authority figures, and no room is big enough to contain them both. However, I have had amazing relationships with two producers that were productive and mutually challenging. The bottom line was that we respected each other, and whatever disagreements we had produced better solutions.

Your skills as a communicator begin when the producer wants to know:

1. Your Understanding of the Play.   There will be a discussion of the story, the plot, and how it was put together. A discussion of other works by or about the author will probably ensue. How does this play fit in, or is it a departure? What does each of us think about the play, and more particularly are we in agreement about what work has to be done and what should be left alone? What elements are best for the play, meaning who should we cast, what designers and other personnel? Who's right for it and who's wrong, based on what we understand the play to be?

2. How Strong You Are in Your Viewpoint Right Now.   Your preparation has led you to a "working" idea of what the play is about. Your entire process, from getting the assignment to opening night, is exploring, locating, and clearly delivering to the audience what the play is about. But if you don't know what the core of the play is or have only a vague idea about how to do the play, it's fairly certain that you will not be given what you think you need to do the production, let alone the job.

Example

You are directing *A Doll's House*. What's this play about? There are many possibilities. But just as an actor can't play more than one thing at a time, the director finally has to pull together the entire production on one strong idea. Otherwise, the director is saying:

- I don't have a strong idea.
- Why do I have to commit until I've started rehearsals?
- I have a strong idea, kind of, but I may want to change it for something else after I get going.

If you change your mind as the sets and costumes are being built, a great deal of time and money will have gone down the drain. If you switch acting styles or make sudden adjustments in the performances, the actors will be confused and insecure when playing for an audience. You will be perceived as unable to make up your mind. Your team will feel that today's work means tomorrow's changes, so why put anything into it?

On the other hand, a director must have the latitude to make changes because work on a production is a growing, moving, living thing. But each time a change is made, you must convince all those involved that it is a change that brings the play closer to what it's about. Otherwise you are spinning out notions and caprices, and everyone around you is quietly losing confidence in the collaboration.

3. How You See It.   "What's the concept?" That's everyone's question to the director. "Are we doing *A Doll's House* on ice skates, or changing Norway to Malibu in the 1950s? Are we playing it 'straight,' or do you have 'a new hook' into it?" Unfortunately the word *concept* has come to mean scenery and the externals of physical production. But these externals are developed from what everyone believes to be the internal life of the play. Sadly, so much emphasis has lately been given to concept that production values have become more important than the play itself. Many so-called high-concept productions are done for the sake of themselves without any meaning or content other than their own decorative glitz. The producer may be into glitz. Many are. If so, you're in business.

But glitz costs money. The more "conceptual" a production is, the more expensive it's bound to be. You'll hear talk of "film" "multimedia," "live musicians," "ever-changing scenery," "stylized costumes," "masks," "animals," "pyrotechnics," "dancers in special choreography," and so forth. The director should find out early in the game what the producer's budget really is. The director has to ask if the cost of the concept is going to mean that no money will be left to hire good actors and if this concept is going to take so much rehearsal and tech time to pull off that there will never be enough time to work on the performances.

The Designers

The director collaborates with three designers: sets, costumes, and lights. If you consider sound, there can be a fourth designer. Each is a different relationship. There can be a good deal of friction on the university level between the designers and the director. The director tends to come in with a concept all laid out and uses the set designer as a glorified draftsman. "Here's the set. I'd like it just like this only bigger." This makes the set designer feel useless and very resentful. There's been no collaboration, no process, and why should the designer put her name on what is essentially the director's set?

On the other hand, you hear directors complain, "I don't know what to do with my designer. She's put all kinds of things in the set I hate and don't want. What should I do?" Tell her! "She won't listen." Tell her again! "I'm afraid to. She goes ballistic on me all the time."

In both cases there's been no communication, let alone a collaboration. The set designer and the director do their best work when they have spent time together, talking, exchanging ideas, and examining rough sketches before making any decisions. It once took me and a designer four months to figure out where the main entrance of the room should be. Everything depended on the placement of that entrance—laughs, timing, rhythm. It was a great joy to us when we got it right because that entrance became a special service to the play.

When you have a very strong idea about the set or see very vivid images, it can be helpful to the designer. You might see the work of a certain artist and say, "It reminds me of Edward Hopper." But the designer has to have the privilege of your treating her like an artist, one whose originality and ingenuity are respected. She may give you Edward Hopper, but in her own way. Don't ask her to give an exact replica. In that case you don't need a designer, you need a technician.

The big questions in this collaboration are: "What do we want to show onstage? What do we want the audience to see? What do we eliminate?"

Costume designers, right from the start, always want to work much more specifically than the set designer. They seem to require many more details than the director is prepared to give immediately. It's too bad we can't have the luxury of rehearsing for a few months, find what the play is really about, then make all these decisions. All we can do is make major decisions before we see what we have on stage and come in on a wing and a prayer.

There are two ways of working with costumes. One is to create a look that you and the designer think is right. The other is to develop ideas based on the actors who are playing the roles. I prefer the latter way. If Actress X is playing so and so, and I know she looks bad in green, I won't put her in green. If she's kind of hard edged, but the character is soft and vulnerable, I'll look to the designer to help her with a costume that will heighten the qualities the role needs. But there is a danger in working this way. You have to do what is best for the actress as the character and not permit the actress to do what is best for herself.

The lighting designer comes in at the last minute and has about two days to hang, focus, and give you something by the technical rehearsal. The discussions between the two of you are very important prior to going into production. Not to be cynical, but you want to ascertain that the designer has read the play. You also want to make sure that there is coordination on all fronts: sets, costumes, and lighting. And you must arrange for the lighting designer to see several run-throughs and spend time after each, sharing ideas. If the director wants complicated lighting with many cues and many different effects, tech time will be needed. It's not advisable to have your actors wait around while you and the designer go through intricate lighting details. It's enervating and takes you away from their performances. The wisest thing is to schedule lighting rehearsals without the actors. The director should always make sure that these rehearsals are built in as part of the production schedule.

With the advent of computer technology, lighting design is on the verge of being done on a computer screen with a replica of the set, enabling the director and designer to choose color, intensity, and exact cues before going into the theatre.

I've always found the design team members quite invaluable during techs, dresses, and previews, not only for the work they do, but also for their comments on what they are watching. To a certain extent, the designers have lived with the play almost as long as the director has, but they have had the advantage of not being in rehearsals daily. They come in with great objectivity, and their advice and opinions are invaluable. There's also a family atmosphere, a feeling of "we're all in this together" as you sit in the theatre together to watch what you've all created come together onstage. And when things get rough and seem absolutely disastrous, you'll invariably have a good laugh together, which helps everyone get through.

The Technical Staff

Everyone looks to the director to be prepared: the stage managers, technical director, and wardrobe and prop people. They do their job by asking you questions whenever they can get a hold of you because they have a very limited amount of time to get their end of things done. They look upon the director as the most prepared person on the project, the person who will make the final decisions from what they have selected to show you. If you're not prepared, you'll want everything, in which case it will be clear that you don't know what you want. You'll be like the coach of a team giving ten different game plans at once—not a recipe for leadership. If your research has included the gathering of articles, pictures, and books, share it with them. In many cases these people have done their research, too. Take time to discover what it is. It may be just the thing you need or something useful that you hadn't thought of.

The Dramaturg

Dramaturgy is a fairly recent development in the American theatre. It has been practiced in Europe, however, since the eighteenth century. On the few occasions that I've had to use a dramaturg, I've found the experience to be a mixed blessing, neither completely fulfilling nor completely disappointing. I do look forward to a time when I will have a more rewarding experience because I know many people who have. Leon Katz, who is professor emeritus of Yale University and now teaches advanced history, literature, and text analysis at UCLA, has contributed the following article on dramaturgy, which pretty much sums up what it is, what the difficulties in the creative collaboration are between the dramaturg and everyone else, and what obvious benefits a good relationship can have on a show.

Dramaturgy in Brief
by Leon Katz
I

Criticism is concerned with what a play is.
Dramaturgy is concerned with what a play might become.

The critic is focused on the completed play and production.
The dramaturg is focused on the process of creating the play and production.

The critic's work begins on opening night.
The dramaturg's work begins weeks if not months in advance of rehearsals.

II

Dramaturgs have multiple functions—though rarely if ever are they all relevant to a single production or to a single theatre's employment:

1. Advising artistic directors on their choice of plays, the shape of their seasons, and the artistic direction of their theatre in general.
2. Absent a literary manager, reading submitted plays and hunting out feasible plays for production.
3. Translating and/or adapting plays for production.
4. Working with playwrights on the development of their plays.
5. Working with directors on preparation for rehearsals (breakdown of script, production concept, and so forth).
6. Providing director with background material—historical, biographical, pictorial, literary, glossary, and so forth—whatever would be useful and relevant for the director during rehearsal process.

(Items 5 and 6 are sometimes accomplished, by especially ambitious and capable dramaturgs, in a *dramaturg's protocol,* a document prepared well in advance of rehearsals, composed of the research material mentioned earlier, a detailed script analysis, and a production concept either previously agreed upon with the director or contributed as suggestion.)

7. During rehearsals, holding regularly scheduled note sessions with the playwright and the director, providing ongoing *in-house* critiques of the development of play and production.
8. Writing program notes orienting audiences to special aspects, as necessary, of the play and/or production.

All more easily said than done.

III

Obviously, the heart of the dramaturg's contribution is working with the director and the playwright. In both instances, the *don'ts* are as important as the *dos.*

Dos

1. First and foremost, earning the trust of the playwright and the director. Neither, initially, has any reason to suppose that the opinion of the dramaturg has any more validity than their own. The dramaturg who best wins artistic trust offers knowledge, experience, and negotiating skill. To wit:

   - Knowledge: Ideally valuable is a dramaturg who offers thorough backgrounds in languages, history/criticism of drama and theatre, research expertise, and generally, educational, and cultural breadth.
   - Experience: In practical theatre. Ideally useful for playwright and director would be a dramaturg with an impeccable ear, a practiced eye, a sure stage sense, analytic skill, and a heightened awareness of the dramatic and the theatrical. Obviously, these are earned best, though they are unhappily not guaranteed, by personal and in-the-arena experience of directing, acting, playwriting, and even design. Dramaturgs without some such experience can be hampered by defective sense of the theatrically possible and relevant, and so their suggestions could be conceivably beside the point and dismissable.
   - Negotiating: The dramaturg requires skill in manner and style of dealing with playwright and director. A dramaturg has to articulate criticism and offer suggestions without being either too tentative, too self-effacing, or too overbearing, and deal sensitively with the sensibilities of playwright and director, but at the same time must be forthright and persuasive. Very difficult, but an absolute key to usefulness.

2. Prerehearsal work: Ideally (as suggested above), the dramaturg prepares a *dramaturg's protocol*, or in another way formats background information that would be useful to directors, actors, designers. To be sure, these are accustomed to doing this work for themselves. Its value, however, when

offered by the dramaturg well in advance of rehearsals, can be in its greater comprehensiveness, breadth of reference, and professional research expertise.

Over and above the gathering of information, the dramaturg (again, ideally) also does a scene-by-scene script breakdown, analyzing and articulating the structure and dynamic of each scene, and of the play as a whole. The focus of this analysis is on the theatrical and dramatic *function* of scenes rather than on implications of meaning embedded in the text. It is intended to be useful to director and—if the director wishes—the actors in exploring strategies that enhance the playability of the play as a whole and of its individual scenes. Directors tend to feel this exercise to be an invasion of their own domain, but tend too to be surprised by the suggestive value that can emerge from such analyses. And with dramaturgs who have earned their trust, directors find it valuable to work on the script breakdown in collaboration with the dramaturg from the start.

Similarly, the production concept may be prepared by the director alone, or collaboratively with the dramaturg, or may be a dramaturg's suggestion offered to the director. In any case, as in the instance of script breakdown, with mutual trust and respect established between director and dramaturg, the dramaturg's contribution to the production's concept can be significant and valued.

3. Rehearsal work with the director: During rehearsals, the dramaturg should (again, ideally) be a second pair of eyes and ears, and a second critical intelligence, for the director. Dramaturgical notes for the director vary from the merest— pronunciation of words, prop anachronisms, inaudible moments, and so forth—to the most comprehensive—the actors' individual performances, the director's effectiveness in staging a scene, or an act, or the entire play. Examples of some of the larger matters such notes comprehend: Action and dynamic (of scene, act, play)—fully realized? Emotional values (of scene, act, play)—reach maximal effectiveness? Inherent logic

(of scene, act, play)—followed? Moment-to-moment believability (of acting, physical staging, play, production concept)—maintained? And so forth. Clearly, all of these questions are the substance of the director's every waking
moment's concern, and notes of these kinds obviously and
bluntly tread on directorial domain. But the ideal dramaturg
whom this text posits offers a somewhat different, somewhat
more objective, somewhat more disengaged perspective that
can frequently lend more objectivity and clarity to the director's own perspective during his/her close concentration in the
rehearsal process.

In the interest of this relative objectivity and disengagement,
dramaturgical visits to rehearsals should be spaced and
should ideally occur when a unit of work (a major sequence,
a scene, an act) has reached an interim stage of readiness.
Not being involved in each moment of rehearsal work, the
dramaturg may be capable of offering that second perspective that would be of value.

Additionally, the timing of different types of notes can
make a considerable difference in their value to the director.
Simply put, when they're still crawling is the wrong time to
find fault with their inadequate flying. A dramaturg's understanding of the step-by-step, developmental nature of the
rehearsal process and sensitivity to the moment when a kind
of note is relevant and realizable are crucial.

4. Work with the playwright: In this relation, the *don'ts* are
   more important than the *dos* (see below). In an ideal
   playwright's universe, dramaturgical advice is restricted
   to help with these questions: Is it (moment, scene, act,
   play) believable? Logically coherent? Effective (emotionally, dramatically, theatrically)? And does it avoid (see
   below) the pretense on the part of the dramaturg that
   he/she is an arbiter of universal principles of drama and
   the demands of popular taste? The art of working with
   playwrights lies in nurturing the play the playwright
   intended. The questions just listed are geared to help.

Don'ts

1. Relation with actors: None. One, not multiple voices, addresses the actors. Another voice inserting itself between director and actor leads at best to rehearsal chaos and at worst to subversive politics. Dramaturg's notes concerning actors and acting are filtered exclusively through the director.

2. Prerehearsal work with director: Dramaturgical labors on script analysis, technical breakdown of script, production concepts, and so on remain in the realm of suggestions. Should there be a division of opinion on these preliminary matters, the director is necessarily final arbiter. An overly persistent, overly insistent dramaturg, no matter how persuaded of the efficacy of his/her position, quickly becomes a liability. A director's decision, once made, becomes the commitment of both director and dramaturg.

3. Rehearsal work with director: Several major *don'ts*.

   First: The temptation is enormous to step into the critic's sandbox and do notes that are definitively sardonic rather than useful. Almost all notes are at least by implication negative, but the helpful ones are soberly and clearly stated, and—most important of all—attempt to ferret out underlying problems and offer positive, practical suggestions for correction. Satire, parody, and send-up are critics' pleasures, not dramaturgs'.

   Second: What seems to be a ridiculously minor matter is in fact major: the physical positioning of the dramaturg during rehearsals, or, the further back and out of the line of vision of both the director and the actors, the better. A prominent display of scribbling notes all through a rehearsal can be distinctly unnerving to both director and actors, and as a consequence, can subvert their focus. The *don't*: Sitting at the director's side, whispering into his/her ear, holding conference while the actors are on their feet and working, and then scribbling, scribbling. It is the mutual responsibility of dramaturg and director to avoid this distracting perpetual rehearsal confab.

Third: On the other hand, the dramaturg's value is lost to the production if he/she allows private and regularly scheduled sessions with the director to lapse, or, worst of all, allows the director to ignore dramaturgical notes and verbal input altogether. By custom and by habit, directors in American theatre tend still to be suspicious of or threatened or annoyed by the dramaturg's function, and it frequently takes psychological acuity on the dramaturg's part to wean and woo successfully. The *don't*: Don't give up.

4. Work with the playwright: The most important *don't* of all: The dramaturg succumbing to the temptation of, in effect, writing him/herself into the playwright's play. The ultimate test of the dramaturg's skill and objectivity is in the avoidance of turning the play into an expression of his/her own tastes, beliefs, and predilections in the guise of instructing the playwright in "what works." Rather than serving the play's development, it merely adulterates the playwright's intent with an alternate one, and intervenes between the playwright and the play.

The dramaturg who observes all the *dos* goes to dramaturgical heaven; the others are harrowed forever in hell.

FREQUENTLY ASKED QUESTIONS

Q: Is there such a thing as too much preparation?

A: No. But not all that you've discovered through your preparation is usable. Much of it is informational. Know that there is a difference between abstract, intellectual, or theoretical information, which, can be very interesting, but won't play. A student was recently talking about his rehearsals for LeRoi Jones's *Dutchman*. His research included studies in the period (1960s), the civil rights movement, racism in America, and so forth. But he was complaining that he couldn't get the play to work. He thought the characters were symbols for aspects of American society. What he missed was the fact that the play is a primitive ritual in which basic instincts are being touched upon: sex between the races, lust for what is forbidden, tearing down conventionality, succumbing to temptation, and an uncontrollable desire to destroy and kill.

You always have to prepare yourself for the emotional life of the play as much as for its intellectual intent. Trust the audience. It will make those intellectual connections without all your help.

Q: If I hate the new play I'm working on, can I quit?

A: You'll be letting everyone on the team down if you do. Quitting is never something that should be an option. If the writer is in there trying, if he or she is making every effort to make the play better, you have to stay with it. If the writer is not there, if you have been abandoned and can't get the play to work, you should talk the situation over with your producer or advisor. It might be better to close down the production than to abandon it.

Q: The writer makes me nervous. Can I keep him away from rehearsal?

A: Absolutely. But that's not a collaboration, that's warfare. You have to examine yourself: Why are you nervous? Why are you trying to keep him out? There is always a period in rehearsals when I prefer that the writer stay away. It's when I like to improvise and explore with the actors. The writer always gets nervous when his words aren't being used every second. Later I want the writer there to share any problems we may have. I know that if I can't stage something properly, there's a problem with the writing. If an actor is having continual problems making a certain area work, the writer has to be there to see it and solve it.

Q: If the playwright is no longer alive and I could imagine a conversation with him, what questions should I ask?

A: You could ask, "Why did you write this play?" He'd probably answer, "I needed the money at the time," or, "It was five-hundred years ago; how do you expect me to remember?" He might even say, "I wrote it because I was a writer and that's what writers do—they write." The more specific question, "What did this play come out of?" asks what events occurred in the author's life to spark the writing of the play. This can be found by reading biographical material and learning about the history of the particular time the play was written. You don't need to conjure up the author do this. Your main question should be how this play fits into the body of the author's work, or how it's different. If you were studying a certain painting, you would want to know about the painter's work that preceded it: How its subject matter is the same or different? What palette was used to create the painting in question? Is it different in tone, texture, and intensity from earlier works? How is light used? What's being conveyed here? Then you would go into the paintings that followed it and see where it fits in as far as the artist's development is concerned.

If I could imagine a meeting with Shakespeare and I was in the middle of directing one of his comedies, my questions would be:

1. Half of this play isn't funny. Is it supposed to be? What am I missing?
2 Many of the words are obscure and no longer in use today. Would you mind if I changed them or should I leave them alone? Would you mind if I cut them because no one will get them?
3. The scenes are too long. Can I cut them or can I rearrange the text so that two scenes are intercut together?
4. Scholars disagree on the meaning of many lines. What do they mean?
5. You aren't coming to rehearsal are you? You're going to make the actors very nervous.

Whether or not the playwright is alive and well or no longer living, you are his partner and collaborator. You should dig into the play to find its intentions and the best ways of presenting them.

Q: What if I vehemently disagree with the producer on the way something is going?

A: If it's a matter of the budget, you may not get your way. The producer is signing the checks. If it's a matter of what you are doing to a scene in the play, she may disagree, but invariably it's the director's call. She's not going to pull you off the show or take it over necessarily. She'll nag at you and make your life difficult. But by opening night she'll say either, "You were right, and I was wrong," or "I was right, and you should have listened to me."

Q: What if I hate the work that my designers are doing?

A: Don't let it get to the point where you hate it. When you are working with the set designer, ask for rough sketches. Do not let the designer go to a model until you've seen sketches, talked them over, revised them, talked them over again, gotten new ideas, seen new sketches, combined elements from one sketch into the next, and then at last said, "Let's see a model." The same thing with costume designers. The minute that you see beautifully rendered color paintings of all the characters, you know that your mind has been made up for you by the designer. Go through a slow, evolutionary process beforehand.

It's very easy to hate what a lighting designer is doing to the show. Go up to him and tell him. You'll find he'll give you what you want.

Q: I gather I can't change designs midstream. True?

A: You can modify, but you really can't stop the shops after half the set is built and painted. The collaboration between you and the designers has to be such that if you feel you've made an error in judgment, the designers will help you by knowing what can be altered, what can be changed, and how, within what's already been built, things can fit your new idea.

Q: I don't understand dramaturgs. They don't act, they don't write, they don't direct. Why should anyone pay any attention to them?

A: You don't have to. The dramaturg is a resource and can be used as a collaborative partner. The actors are getting only a part of you, so are the designers. The dramaturg can be the only person on a show to whom you can talk about all your ideas and get feed-back. He or she can serve as an additional pair of eyes who see the big picture when most of the time you are like a miniaturist, stuck on one tiny detail at a time.

CHAPTER SEVEN

WORKING WITH ACTORS

You can do without scenery, without much lighting, and for costumes you can always use street clothes. There are all sorts of ways you can eliminate production values. You can also eliminate the playwright by doing a published script or, better yet, one that is in the public domain. But unless you are going to use puppets, you are stuck with actors.

Actors come in various sizes and various degrees of difficulty or cooperation. There are actors who want to be told what to do but not how to do it. There are other actors who want to be told exactly how to do it. And there are actors who don't want to be told much of anything, except that they are wonderful.

No matter the temperament or ego of the actor, the director must make the collaboration work. Just as musicians test every new conductor, actors will test the director. They want to see if you really know your stuff, if you have a vision of the play, if you are flexible or rigid, if they can do what they think should be done with the role, or if you'll be a help or an impediment. All this testing is really motivated by the actors' wanting to find out whether they can trust you or not. It may be all right for you to ask an actor to touch his right elbow with his right hand or to play the scene standing on his head, but although the actor may be seemingly compliant, he's thinking, "I'm going to be out there in front of an audience doing this? Is this going to work, or am I going to look like a horse's ass? Is this director leading me down a blind alley?"

When does the actor begin to trust the director? When he sees that what you are asking him to do works. When is that? Sometimes that's not until previews. Hopefully it's much sooner in the process. That little flash of recognition in the actor's mind that he's in good hands may happen in the first rehearsal, or somewhere in the middle of blocking, or notes after a run-through, or not at all. But you'll know when it happens. It's a great psychological relief to the director because you know you've solidified what can be an amazing relationship.

It's important to understand that the actor, although testing you in an attempt to trust you, is very rarely judging you. He's too subjectively involved to sit back and determine if you have any talent, if you are adequate for the job, if what you are doing is good enough. Instead, the actor is too busy looking for you to judge him — "How am I doing? Am I on the right track? Do you want more? Do you think I ought to do less? Am I good in the role or lousy?" Also, actors tend to look to the bright side: "This director is weird, but he may be on to something," "I hate the way she works, but I respect her intellect," "I've never worked this way before, but it may be good for me."

It's only when the director compounds his own insecurity with the mistaken notion that he's being judged that he flares up and targets the actor as enemy. You can't beat trust out of an actor. You have to earn it.

AUDITIONING

Many directors use auditions to figure out what they want. They are at the smorgasbord of life, sampling, discarding, indulging indiscriminately. They use auditions primarily to make up their minds. "I'll know what I want for this play when I see it." The other approach is the director who wants to be entertained in the audition. "The person who excites me the most, moves me, makes me laugh, is the one I'm going to cast." Each type of director is channel surfing, or window shopping, going from one actor to the next in order to become inspired enough to find someone who's going to hit him just right. But an audition is not the place to make up your mind what you're looking for or to be entertained. Although if either happens, you can regard it as an unexpected bonus.

There is a certain formality at an audition that helps the process.

1.   The director should introduce himself and whoever is with him in the room. That could be the author, the producer, any of the stage managers, and so forth. Every effort should be made to be cordial. You have your job, the actor is hoping to get his.

2. Whether or not you make small talk before the audition, afterward, or not at all is not important. But you should thank the actor for coming in.

3. If the actor is to read from the play with someone, such as the stage manager, have the actor's chair positioned so that she is favored and not upstaged by the reader.

4. If you want to stop to make suggestions or have the actor read again with certain adjustments, it will help him. This gives you a chance to sense how receptive the actor is and how well he takes your note. You might even want to improvise with the actor.

5. While the actor is working, those who are observing owe her the courtesy of listening, not reading, talking with each other, or eating.

6. It's sometimes a good idea to have requested the actor to prepare additional material such as two short monologues in order for him to give you an opportunity beyond reading a scene from a play that he may not be too familiar with. If you choose to ask for a monologue, make sure that you state up front if you want him to play to you or away from you.

7. When the audition is over, and even if it's been the worst thing you've ever seen in your life, I think it's important that you don't hurt the actor, who is very vulnerable at this moment, and that you help her with a decent exit. "Thank you for coming, I appreciate it" coming from you will help her get out of the room.

8. Make notes on each actor because at the end of the day you have to make an assessment, usually with the author and the producer.

9. In a professional situation the producer is the top of the hierarchy. He has raised the financing and is responsible to his investors. He or she does the hiring. It is a matter of protocol that the director consults with the producer on final casting and that the producer make the job offers. Under no circumstances should the director ever lead the actor on with "You're the one I want for the part." This invalidates all the other actors waiting in the hallway to audition and negates the producer's ability to negotiate. The director should never say to an actor at the end of the day, "The part is yours." Your mind

may change or be changed. Also, you can't discount the actor's feelings: the actor may not really want the part after auditioning. If you are in a school situation, the chairman or the area heads have to be consulted on casting. To help you make up your mind, conduct callbacks. This enables you to hear more of the actor, perhaps in other scenes from the play, and gives you a chance to work together more. It's often valuable to hear the opinions of other people on your team about a particular actor. Actors Equity Association has a rule about how many times you may call an actor back without paying him.

10. Be aware of how many actors are waiting in the hallway. This will help you judge how much time to spend with each person. In any case, it's courteous to allow the actor to finish whatever piece she's doing. Cutting her off in the middle of a scene or monologue and throwing her out of the room is unnecessary. Have patience.

The audition should serve the following functions:

1. Unless it's a dance audition, what's really going on for the director is listening. You want to hear how responsive the actor is to the music of the play. If the actor is not responsive, but you like the actor's work, you have to either sacrifice that actor or somehow divine that the author's language is going to be eventually mastered and delivered. Not every actor is good for every play. There are excellent actors I wouldn't put in a Shaw play, and as much as I love their work I wouldn't put some in a play by John Guare, who demands very particular cadences and intonation from his characters. You are trying to see if the writing and the actor match up. But beware! There are actors who are very skillful at first readings and get worse thereafter. They're what I call radio actors. They have an immediate sense of the text, but never get better beyond that. How do you make sure that you don't have a radio actor? Ask him to make some adjustments immediately. Deprogram him with radical suggestions and call him back.

2. You have to ask, "Is this a person I want to spend the next couple of months with?" Does the person seem flexible or rigid? Does the person fit into the way you like to work?

What's the person like physically? Can she move? Is she physically free? "Perhaps I'd better improvise something with her and find out." "This one is tense beyond belief. Can I free him of that? Is there enough time?" In short, you are looking for someone with whom you would enjoy working.

3. Oddly enough, the question, "Is the actor right for the role?" is not first on the list. If the actor is a good actor, talented and well trained, someone with whom you'd like to work and who can adapt to the author's language, he or she is worth great consideration. What many directors forget in auditions when they're looking for Mr. Right is that they are looking at actors, who by their very nature will in time be able to transform themselves into the role. Obviously if there are enormous physical disparities between the actor and the character—everyone in the play refers to the character as "Big Daddy," but the actor is under five feet tall and weighs ninety pounds—there's a problem. In general, however, unless it bends the play out of shape, you have much more latitude between the concept of the character you may have in your mind and the talent that is standing before you in the audition room.

4. I knew a director who was quite startled when someone casually mentioned, "Both your leads have lisps." He never heard it until it was mentioned. Well, you might say, if he didn't hear it, maybe the audience members didn't hear it, but they did. That is when the actors spoke loud enough to be heard because both also had faulty voice projection and couldn't get past the fifth row. The director didn't hear this problem because he knew the text so well that he was hearing it even when it wasn't audible to others. Check speech problems and ascertain vocal training.

5. In many auditions someone is pushing someone. The producer has a payback to someone's wife, the author met someone that day in a train station who helped carry his bag and turned out to be an actor. You might have a few of them yourself. These "courtesy" auditions are a fact of life. But the success of a show is largely determined by the way it's cast. In all occasions you need to do what you believe is right for the play.

6. If you are in a school situation, auditioning is different because your casting pool is limited, and actors are there to learn just as much as you are. You are obliged to give roles as part of their training.

REHEARSALS

Now that it has begun, you and the actors are together for five, six, eight, ten, twelve hours a day until the play opens and beyond that if the play runs. The director must always keep one thing in mind: "I'm going to get what I want." This is assuming that you know what you want. The art is how you go about getting what you want from the actor. Tyrone Guthrie tried everything with an actor who was getting worse and worse. Toward the end of rehearsal the actor complained that he didn't know what he was doing. Guthrie said, "Be a cello!" All at once everything clicked, and the actor knew how to play his character. An actor I was working with had a bad habit of fragmenting his lines. I tried to tell him to pick up his cues, to accelerate his speeches, to stop taking so many pauses, and so forth. Nothing worked. Finally the producer suggested that I tell the actor to "tie his ends together." It made no sense to me, but I told him. He said, "What? I have loose ends?" And immediately he tightened up all his speeches. So the issue is semantic. It's how we put things. But the director must remain undaunted. Doggedly you pursue your vision of the play, never giving up, especially on the actors. You try everything to get it to work. Don't think of difficulties as obstacles. Think of them as challenges.

First Rehearsal

Traditionally this is your "first reading" together. Everyone should be there—actors, designers, producers, author, stage managers, tech staff, publicity people, everyone connected to the show. Some directors like to give speeches to warm things up, others save their talk until the reading is over. Some have very little to say. It's all a matter of personal style, and there's no right or wrong in the matter.

The secret of the first reading is that it lets you know — among other things, naturally — what acting problems you're going to have.

Actor A jumps into every cliché in the book.

Actor B pushes.

Actor C is slow and tends to be sentimental.

Actor D already has figured out his characterization, and it's all wrong.

Actor E doesn't listen.

Actor F is perfect. They all should be like her. Actually, her reading is telling me what this play is about. Thank you!

You show the actors the model of the set and the costume sketches. Make sure that each actor has seen his sketch because if the actor has other ideas he'd like to share with you, do it now, not after the costume is built. Make sure that the actors are aware of any special coaching that you have in store for them, such as fight scenes, duels, acrobatics, dances, and dialects.

Some directors talk at great length and elicit comments and questions from the actors about their feelings and observations concerning the play, their characters, or anything that comes to mind. This is called "table work," which has many advantages, obviously, but how much time you have until opening determines how long you're going to spend at the table.

Some directors will call for a five-minute break after the first reading and start blocking. I have to confess that I'm one of those. I feel that I don't know what I'm doing until the play is staged. Staging gives life and breath to the play, to the actors, and to me. I have, however, after staging the play and almost toward the last weeks of rehearsal, sat the cast down, got out our scripts, which the actors have memorized, and had them read off the printed page again. Invariably a revelation or two happens. We'll realize that certain words have been missed, that an actor has been saying something in two sentences when it was written as one, thereby changing the rhythm and timing of the line, that a little stage direction that we all neglected clears up a moment that hasn't been working too well, and in general that we are taking a fresh look at the score, even though we are in the midst of playing its music.

You have to find out which is the best way for you. But again, time is the dominating factor here. If you are in a regional theatre company that has seven weeks of rehearsal you have to hold the actors back. There is no sense in getting the play to work too early: it will be stale by opening night. In a commercial theatre production you have four weeks, usually, until technicals, and in college theatre productions you have the same amount or less to mount a production.

Exploring What the Actor Needs

Actors need an objective eye, they need your help. Whatever you give them, always make sure that it's specific. Tyrone Guthrie's suggesting that an actor be a cello is extremely specific when it comes late in the rehearsal and after many ways of playing a scene had been tried. Had it been said early on, it would be a very general note and confusing to the actor.

There is a school of thought that believes that the director/actor relationship should be very general. That is, the actor should be free to explore various facets of his character. This means that the director should take a back seat and allow the actor to feel his way through scenes, trying different things such as pieces of staging, improvising around the lines, moving wherever and whenever the impulse takes him. If this is acceptable, the director might benefit from this looseness or general approach. What you're really doing is winding the actor up like a top and letting him spin as he will. You are permitting the actor to do a particular kind of investigation that can also benefit you. For example, you might say, "Okay, the next time you do the scene, find some behavior that reflects what your character really thinks about his mother." And the actor might very well find a very interesting way of displaying it. Not all actors like working this way, and not all directors feel that they have the time for it. But every actor works differently and has different needs. The director, very early in rehearsals, has her tentacles out, trying to intuit the best way to work with each actor.

I always enjoy an actor who wants to be creative and to use me as a guide as this kind of exploration of character and circumstance is taking place. It has never threatened me because in the end, either through this process or by later imposing my own ideas, I know I'll get what I want. At a certain point, you have to say, "Enough of this exploring. We're going to set the show now, and of all the things we've found, these are the ones we're going to use." The actor is looking for you to have the final edit.

The director has to be very careful not to fall into a trap when the actor is asking for freedom, but it's a freedom to work out his acting process. There is a big difference between exploring the character and exploring your acting process. The director has to determine what's going on. If the actor is using rehearsing to learn the lines, identify with the character, work on sense memory, or find a way of working on the script, the director is in trouble. This actor will never find the character and how that character fits into the play. This problem is most acute in schools where the actor is learning a process and keeps telling the director, "Don't push me for results!"

In the school situation there are at least two processes going on: the actor's and the director's. Each person has to be patient with the other. The director needs the actor to try his ideas, and the actor needs the director to let her affect what she's been learning in class to work in rehearsals. The director is a surrogate teacher (in a way, he's always a teacher) and has to help the actor bridge her process into performing a role.

A rehearsal is a transaction of agreements and concessions. It's the foundation of collaboration. Concession, by the way, doesn't mean compromise. The director has to concede that the actor is just trying his process out, and the actor has to understand that he must, at the same time, give the director the results that are being asked for. The character is crying at a certain moment. The actor decides to use sense memory to recall the death of her mother. This gets her crying. Usually. Now it doesn't work for some reason. She tells the director that she'll cry when she's found something to cry about. She doesn't want to "push" her process. The director, patient saint that she is, forbears and tells the actress, "Why don't you cry based on what the character is feeling?" The actress says she hasn't found that fully yet and doesn't want to indicate, which is to externalize an emotion that is not felt. The director says, "Just cry. You're an actress! I have to see how it works in terms of the scene and how it will affect everyone else on the stage."

"You mean you want me to cry on cue like some Pavlovian animal?"

"Yes. Actors cry on cue."

Comes the cue, the actress cries, quite effectively. How she did it, what she finally used to make it happen, is not your concern because she got the moment to work. And you know what? The actress is pleased that she is servicing the play by technically fulfilling her role and can go home and work out how she can fill it emotionally to her own satisfaction.

Playing specifics

The text is like a musical score. It has been specifically written and must be specifically played. It will permit interpretation, coloration, atmosphere, mood, and character nuance. But its characters are in the play for a particular reason, and each character is pursuing different things. No matter how you work as a director, you and the actors have to come to terms with the details of the play.

Together you must tackle the following:

1. Character objectives.   What does the character want? Does the character want something throughout the course of the play, or does the want change? The director and the actor have to work together to answer these questions. Sometimes, however, the director, when talking in these terms, tends to be very intellectual, and the actor tends to be very amorphous and vague. What the character wants is often a hard question to answer, but it is the actor's quest, which has to be assisted by the director's help and prodding. Because a good play is rich in incident and complication, it's not always so easy to get to what the character wants. What does Hedda Gabler want? You might say, "She wants to be a man!" but that's not really playable. Not literally, at least. She certainly envies men: their freedom of choice in the world, their economic independence, the fact they can live dangerously, have adventure, carry pistols, win the world. Being a woman is her obstacle. Or is it? Can she use her sex to her advantage? What is it that really drives her throughout the play? What gives her energy and passion? What's her quest? What's the motor that the author has built inside her that makes her go? The director and the actor have to dig in and get to the bottom of what Hedda wants, not only in each scene, but also throughout the course of the play.

You can look at a Pinter play and say, "Who the hell knows what any of those strange characters wants?" The point is that you have to find out. And if it's not clear, the director and the actor have to supply a subtext, that is, a story underneath the lines, that makes it playable for the actor. Even if the audience is not sure, the actor has to be. Even if it's debatable and mysterious to each person who has seen the play, the actor has made specific choices for himself. Otherwise, the actor does not know what he's doing, plays in generalities, and, worse, goes from one emotional affect to the next.

In a rehearsal for Pinter's *The Birthday Party*, the actor playing Stanley couldn't find his character's objective. He had no rationale for why he was at this seaside rooming house, why he reacted the way he did to the strange visitors, why he went to pieces by the end of the play. One day the actor began autoerotic behavior that was shocking. I thought he'd lost his mind. He did this throughout the run-through, and when it was over he asked me if I'd noticed what he was doing. I told him that I had and wondered if he planned on doing this in front of the audience. He said, "No. I found what I was looking for. I found that Stanley wants to hide out of shame, out of fear of being caught, and feels he deserves to be punished when he is caught. Stanley operates out of guilt." We don't know if this was Pinter's intention, which is very opaque, but it worked for the actor. The actor found that playing the need to hide and wanting to escape punishment worked for him. And it worked for the play. Of course, the audience never knew how the actor arrived at any of this.

Every human being wants something. Every character in a play wants something. What makes a play dramatic is the fact that what the character wants is obstructed by obstacles that he has to overcome, and those obstacles create conflict on stage. Obstacles can come from other characters, from circumstances, or from within the character himself.

Every rehearsal must culminate in the actor and director getting closer to what the character is pursuing. The actor always needs the director's help with this. That's why the director who sits back and waits to be entertained never will be—because she hasn't helped the actor get to the core of the role. A play is a collection of characters who want different things and are continually colliding with each other. When Charles Ludlam played Hedda Gabler for me, we had trouble not making the character a ghoul, willful, mean, determined to get what she was after and nasty to everyone around her. We asked, "What does she really want?" We were in performance when Charles said, "I finally found it. Hedda is a coward! She wants everyone around her to act because she hasn't the guts to. She wants the courage to control her life. She finally believes her suicide is her one brave act." He found the hook that he needed in the final performances of the play. The character's wanting courage became so immediate, so poignant, so vital that the production took on a new life, and the play careened forward at an amazing pace.

2. Actions.   If the objective is what the character wants, actions are what he's doing to get what he wants. Action is the "to do" part of acting. It is what the actor plays line by line. Actions are the character's strategy or tactic or approach to obtain the objective. If I want you to give me back money you owe me, my first action might be to ask for it. You might tell me that you don't have the money right now. I've already asked you for it, so I'm not going to play that action again; it's redundant. If I really need the money back, I have to try another approach. I would impress upon you the fact that you promised to pay me back some time ago. My action in that case is to make you feel uneasy and guilty about breaking your promise. You tell me that times have been rough and that you intend to pay me back the first chance you get. I might become very angry, which provokes me into another line of attack: "I don't think you ever intend to pay me back." My action here is to bring the situation to a head and get a commitment from you. You get upset and start showing me your bills and tell me about the troubles you've gone through lately. I say, "Okay, whenever you can." My action is to let you know that I don't like going away empty handed but that I feel sorry for you, yet I expect this debt to be resolved.

I could have just stood there and said over and over, "I want the money you owe me," but that would not have been a very interesting scene, would it? It's the same in plays. Characters are as interesting as their actions that come out of moment-to-moment responses to the situation.

A character can go through an entire repertoire of actions in a single scene, and it's up to the director to guide the actor through as many as possible. The reason why scenes become lifeless and dull is because the actor and the director have not chosen actions, which means that the actor isn't playing anything. Each character wants something and usually wants it now, which is what gives the play its immediacy. As part of now, "no" cannot be taken as an answer. Something is always at stake for the character, which is why the objective has to be fulfilled on stage today, not tomorrow. That's why the character tries everything, does everything to get what she's after.

As an example of actions, let's look at a section of Romeo and Juliet's balcony scene. Both characters, who met briefly at a masked ball, believe that they are in love with each other. It is night, and we are in the Capulets' orchard, where Romeo has been hiding, staring up at Juliet's balcony, when she appears. She confesses that she does not understand why his name has to be Montague, an enemy of her family. Why can't he get rid of that name and take her instead: "Deny thy father and refuse thy name; / Or, if thou wilt no, be but sworn my love, / And I'll no longer be a Capulet." In other words, she's already willing to marry him. He hears this and jumps from his hiding place.

Romeo: I take thee at thy word,
Call me but love, and I'll be new baptized:
Henceforth I never will be Romeo.

Juliet: What man art thou, that, thus bescreened in night,
So stumblest on my counsel?

Romeo: By a name
I know not how to tell thee who I am.
My name, dear saint, is hateful to myself
Because it is an enemy to thee.
Had I it written, I would tear the word.

Juliet: My ears have yet drunk a hundred words
Of thy tongue's offerings, yet I know the sound.
Art thou not Romeo, and a Montague?

Romeo: Neither, fair maid, if either thee dislike.

Juliet: How camest thou hither, tell me, and wherefore?
The orchard walls are high and hard to climb,
And the place death, considering who thou art,
If any of my kinsmen find thee here.

Romeo: With love's light wings did I o'erperch these walls;
For stony limits cannot hold love out,
And what love can do, that dares love attempt.
Therefore thy kinsmen are no stop to me.

Juliet: If they do see thee here, they will murder thee.

Romeo: Alack, there lies more peril in thine eye
Than twenty of their swords! Look thou but sweet,
And I am proof against their enmity.

Juliet: I would not for the world they saw thee here.

Romeo: I have night's cloak to hide me from their eyes;
And but thou love me, let them find me here.
My life were better ended by their hate
Than death prorogued, wanting of thy love.

It's very clear that these characters want one thing: each other. There are no greater urgency and immediacy than love of this kind. However, Shakespeare has put several obstacles in the way of these characters' fulfillment of their objective. Their families are sworn enemies. Romeo puts his life at stake being in the orchard because if he's caught he will be murdered. And they are separated, he on the ground, she on her balcony. What they do to overcome their obstacles and to get what they are after are their actions.

Romeo has overheard Juliet offer herself to him. He leaps from his hiding place and says, "I take thee at thy word, / Call me but love, and I'll be new baptized: / Henceforth I never will be Romeo." What specifically is the actor playing at that moment? What action, what's he doing? He knows that she wants him. His action could be to let her know that she can have him. Just call him "love," he's ready for it.

Now you'll notice that I just said that "his action could be . . ." This is to respect other possibilities. Everything I'm saying is open to other interpretations. I have mine right now, and you'll have yours. But we have to start from somewhere in order to find the details we need to play the scene.

Juliet sees that her musings have been overheard and says, "What man art thou, that, thus bescreened in night, / So stumblest on my counsel?" She's been caught. Does she know it's Romeo? He's said he is, but he could be anyone pretending to be the man she's professed to love. Her action is to make him declare his identity, but Romeo, seizing the chance to play around poetically and philosophically with who he is, uses this as a chance to directly woo her: "By a name / I know not how to tell thee who I am. / My name, dear saint, is hateful to myself / Because it is an enemy to thee. Had I it written, I would tear the word." It's also interesting to note that he begins his direct wooing of her by referring to her as "dear saint," which elevates his intentions into something more lofty than immediately sexual.

Knowing who he is without question, Juliet, although flattered by his line of wooing, is telling him that she's already familiar with it: "My ears have yet drunk a hundred words / Of thy tongue's offerings, yet I know the sound." But she asks, "Art thou not Romeo, and a Montague?" The action of that line could be to put up a wall of resistance against his flowery attempts at seduction.

Romeo will transform himself into anything she likes: "Neither, fair maid, if either thee dislike."

But she feels that they must confront who he is because of the danger: "How camest thou hither, tell me, and wherefore? / The orchard walls are high and hard to climb, / And the place death, considering who thou art, / If any of my kinsmen find thee here."

Again, Romeo, in love with the adventure of the moment, shows her how bold, daring, and crazy about her he is: "With love's light wings did I o'erperch these walls; / For stony limits cannot hold love out, / And what love can do, that dares love attempt.
/ Therefore thy kinsmen are no stop to me."

Admiring his bravura, she feels that some note of reality ought to be injected: "If they do see thee here, they will murder thee."

Romeo has given over to complete abandon and uses her fear to flatter her: "Alack, there lies more peril in thine eye / Than twenty of their swords!" Flattering her, what he's now doing is showing her that she and she alone can protect him: "Look thou but sweet, / And I am proof against their enmity."

He's going too far, and she needs to protect him: "I would not for the world they saw thee here."

Once again, Romeo uses the situation to find poetry to dazzle her with: "I have night's cloak to hide me from their eyes; / And but thou love me, let them find me here."

He admits the degree of his desire for her: "My life were better ended by their hate / Than death prorogued, wanting of thy love."

These are examples of actions that the actors are playing. Some people refer to actions as *intentions*. It's what the character is intending by saying the line. Others might say it's the *subtext* of the lines. Again, semantics.

Actions are what the actors are playing. They are active, needful, and immediate. If the actor is playing actions you will find that the scene has a definite progression and variety. When the actor is not playing actions, he is generalizing, and in Shakespeare that's deadly. It produces affected, rhetorical speech and empty lyricism. The director has to be on his toes and see where the actor can be helped in choosing the most effective actions.

A professional actor can go from one action to the next like a master violinist tearing through a cadenza. Student actors take a lot of time mastering the technique for a number of reasons: (a) It's new to them, (b) rehearsal is only one part of their day, and they tend not to fully retain the work from the night before and (c) actions take enormous concentration and energy, whereas slipping back to old habits of generalizing is easy and always "seems comfortable." (Always beware of the actor who is looking to be comfortable or who declares, "I'm comfortable with this" or "I don't feel comfortable with that." When the actor is "comfortable," he's usually not challenging himself but rather reverting to things that are easy for him.)

Many directors say, "Don't tell me I'm going to have to go through the whole script with every actor this way!" I've never understood that complaint. That's what directing is: going through the details, leaving no stone unturned. However, you don't have to do it all at once. After you begin working with the actors on their actions, they will follow by doing work on their own, if they haven't already. If there is a patch of dialogue that you feel needs to be made specific, do it. Sometimes, however, things sort themselves out without your help. That patch of dialogue may get specific in a day or two without you. Or you may have given the actor so much direction that you sense that she needs a bit of respite from you. In that case, cool it. Maybe in a tech rehearsal you can bring the section up as you are waiting for a light cue together, or you might drop into the dressing room and say, "Oh, by the way, that section at the end of the act has gotten a little general."

But you don't give up. Just find the right moment to get the detail in.

Finally, actions evolve. You can develop the playing of a scene in a very particular way, but after taking a look at it, you might say, "Let's try a different action here, a stronger one there, a more subtle one on the last line." That's why the sooner you get specific, the more time you have to experiment with changes.

3. Rhythm.   The director always hopes that when the show is put together the rhythms will be there with great variety, color, and surprise. You imagine that if all the work you've done is right, the show will find its music. Often it does. Often it does not. You can see many productions that have no flow, no dynamic. There are reasons for this. One is that the cast and director have been reverential to the material in the wrong way. For example, Ibsen and Brecht have been academically pronounced as "important" playwrights. So the actors deliver each sentence as though every word were dipped in bronze. A sententious delivery pervades. Every idea, every word is underlined. The director shouldn't be a party to this. You have to tell your cast members that they aren't performing Ibsen for idiots, that the audience is smart enough to follow the play quicker.

There are some ways that you can break a monotonous or heavy-handed rhythm:

- Tell the actors to "throw away" everything they say. Toss it off, make nothing important.
- Overlap the dialogue. Don't take any pause between cues. Cut in and out of each other like people in real life often do.

- Sit the cast down and work on the rhythm of each section of the play. "You come in louder here. No, louder, smash the scene on your entrance. That's right. Don't play her rhythm, play your own. Don't play in the same mood as the scene before you came on. Come on quicker, keep your dialogue moving." Or, "Slower. Where's the train?"

- Make sure that your actors haven't been using rehearsal to learn their lines and are not delivering their lines in the fragmentary way they learned them. Have periodic speed-throughs when the cast members sit down and rattle off the script as fast as they can. This will keep them on top of the material.

The director must develop a finely tuned ear that hears when the play's rhythms are being observed and when they are being ignored.

Danger: Never play rhythm for the sake of itself. It can make the play hollow and artificial. You want a sense of rhythm, a sense of structure, but always make sure that you are filling in the emotional life as well.

4. Character.   The sum of the actor's choice of objectives, actions, and rhythm is essentially the character's inner behavior. The externals of behavior, the look, the walk, the body language, are what I personally stay out of. I leave that to the actor's creativity in the hope that there will be a metamorphosis by dress rehearsal. I love to be surprised by what the actor has come up with and by how sets, costumes, and lighting help transform him into the character.

I don't dictate or impose a walk, a manner of speech, and so forth. Otherwise, everyone would be running around on stage exactly like me. When I'm directing I may go through a piece of blocking or say a line with the emotional color that that character is going through, but I don't expect to be imitated. As specific as I am with actions, objectives, and rhythm, I'm as loose with how these things should be physicalized because, frankly, I don't know. The actor knows.

Sometimes suggestion of an image can be helpful. Like that "be a cello" line of Tyrone Guthrie. The actor understood that his character's inner music was dark, languorous, and yearning. The image activated him. He was able to physicalize it. Even if you toss out to an actor an image that is not directly usable, it may spark the actor into one that is.

You might find that an animal image might help the actor. If Hedda Gabler is being played like a soap opera, full of pauses and totally ponderous, tell the actress playing the lead that she's a ravenous tiger. Let her go to the zoo to observe one. Let her experiment by playing rehearsals like a tiger who's feeding off everyone. Hedda has a ravenous appetite, nothing satisfies her. The animal study might help the actress.

The director is responsible for seeing that everyone is in the same play. There can be great diversity of characterization, but the director controls how far each actor is to go in terms of style and reality. That's why actors always say, "You're watching, you have to tell me if I'm going too far or not far enough."

5. Improvising in Rehearsal.   If there is a problem with a scene, for example, the director and actors might want to improvise to find a solution. The problem can be with the writing, especially if it's a new play, with the acting, which is not specific enough, or with the direction, which hasn't found what is going on underneath the scene. Problems should never be viewed as, "It's the actors. They're no good." If the actors are no good, it's the direction that's no good. Assigning blame to actors is not taking the responsibility of direction fully. If the actor is wrong, you've cast her and have to make things right by finding adjustments and ways of playing the scenes that work. If the actor gets a bad review, it's really your bad review as well. It's implied that he did what you asked of him. And if an actor gets a rave, paradoxically, you have to expect to get little of the credit.

When you improvise, always do so with a tangible goal in mind because it drives actors crazy when they think the director is either improvising for the sake of itself or trying to use them to find out what the hell he wants. Set the situation of the improv very clearly and tell the cast what you're aiming for, such as:

Intensifying Actions and Objectives

- Often in new plays there will be a character who seems to be hanging around the scene with not much to do. The actor asks himself repeatedly, "Why am I in this scene?" but isn't finding out. The director could set up an improv in which the characters are going through the situation but using whatever words come to mind. You have to make sure that they don't become random and casual, just chatting their way through. Reaffirm what is at stake or why they want what they want now. As a matter of fact, you might tell them to begin anything that they feel compelled to say with the phrase, "I want."

- If the actors are just playing cue to cue with no behavior and very little concentration, if the actors are not in the moment and are working mechanically, try an inner monologue, which demands that they verbalize whatever is going through their character's mind. As the other actor speaks, the actor doing the inner monologue says out loud whatever comes to her mind and improvises around the lines of the text. The monologue keeps her reacting to what is being said and helps trigger her objective. If you try this and find that the actor doesn't know what to say or uses the monologue sparingly, you know you're in trouble. The actor is unresponsive and nonreactive. It also means that she is not willing to fight for what her character wants. I often think of an inner monologue as acting in a film. If you are doing a close-up of an actor who isn't speaking, you are really photographing what is going on inside his head. If nothing is going on you don't have your close-up.

- The actor has to answer: "Where am I coming from? Where am I going? And why now?" You can improvise with the actor the moment that takes him into the scene, trying to capture that impulse that provokes his entrance. All good entrances are made by the character coming onto the scene with a definite purpose. Have the actor or actors do the scene just before their entrance. Sometimes you'll find their work so interesting that you wish it were part of the play.

- You might feel that the actor is playing the role too obviously and hasn't found contrasting colors or other values. If, for instance, you're doing *Hedda Gabler* and find the actress playing her to be more overbearing and turgid each day, you have obviously lost her charm and what makes her magnetic to men. Improvise something silly like Hedda giving Judge Brack a surprise birthday party, where she can be merry and gay and alluring to all the men in the room.

Clarifying Circumstances

- Physical realities often go by the wayside. If you are doing a play like David Rabe's *Hurlyburly*, which is about a group of men in Hollywood who are wrecked on alcohol and drugs and who are paranoid and incapable of having a healthy relationship with a woman, you have to consider the substances that they are using. Two of the characters go off the deep end with their abuse. Take time, find out what these mental states are, and improvise with the actors how this behavior manifests itself other than by just the words that the author has provided. At this point in rehearsal someone will say, "Why don't we get stoned and do the play?" The answer to that is that there is no way that you can do this play or any other while stoned.
- How does the climate affect behavior? How integral is the heat in *Cat on a Hot Tin Roof* or other plays of Tennessee Williams? You see scenes supposedly set in the snow, rain, or storm, and the actors just seem to be on a nice, comfy stage up there. Doesn't the atmosphere play a part in what the characters are after and how they can go about getting it? And if a scene is static or sterile you might want to throw an atmospheric condition into it to give it some texture.
- Are the characters in a new environment or an accustomed one? Is that chair you're sitting on the one you've had your whole life? What does it mean to you? Was it your father's? How do you relate to it? Is the place new to you? What feelings

do you have being here? All this can be developed by improvs. And what you find in the improv can be used to enrich the actual scene.

Improvs are to acting what variations on a theme are to music. They help you expand a central idea or unlock intuitive ones. They free you from the text, yet help you find the text in a more meaningful way. Improvs help the actors and director get connected to the material. And even if some improvs are not directly usable, they provide you with information that you'll be glad you discovered.

Giving Notes

Actors expect notes, and directors are expected to give them. There are, however, a time and a place for everything. Some notes are best given in private, not during the session in front of the whole cast. If I feel that an actor has gone way off, I prefer to tell him privately. I don't want to humiliate him, nor do I want to give him the opportunity to be defensive.

Some notes are premature, and you have to wait until you feel that it's just the right time to give them. You may like the way an actor is working, but it's taking the pace out of the scene. If you demand that she speed it up, you know she's going to just play the pace and cease exploring all the good things that she's bringing to rehearsal. At a strategic moment, when you feel that she's gotten a good foundation but that a quicker pace will help her pull it all together, you give her the note.

Some notes are forgotten because the actor hasn't written them down, thinking he'll remember. If you've got one of those "Sorry, you told me and I forgot" actors, you might give him the written note after you've told him orally.

As a rule, always give notes to actors yourself. Never have an assistant or a stage manager give your notes, unless you are running to catch a plane. You saw the performance, you took the note, what that note means only you know and only you can explain.

CHECKLIST

1. Am I giving the actors a real chance in auditions, or am I locked into preconceived ideas? Am I casting to type or willing to look at things in a more original way?

2. How much do I know about the actor's process? Am I giving him a chance to create the role, or is he taking advantage of me by using rehearsal to do his own work?

3. Have I really got actions and objectives going in the scenes? Objectives should be personal, immediate, and selfish. The character has to want what she wants now. There should be something at stake for everyone. It has to be close to life or death, otherwise, there's no immediacy.

    The actions should be varied. Am I playing things on one note, or is there a logical variety of tactics and approaches to how the characters are achieving their goals?

4. Am I helpful enough to the actors or too interfering? Do my notes seem to work? If not, what other adjustments can I think of? Am I starting to blame my actors and taking less responsibility for the work?

5. When I put the play together, is there any sense of rhythm — rhythms that change, different colors and tones — or is it all on one note? Have I tried a sit-down rehearsal to work on rhythm, timing, and variation?

6. Do the characterizations seem specific enough? How can I help the actors with more interesting choices? Are the characters different than each other, or is everyone playing the same thing?

7. Will improvising help the areas that are weak?

8. Am I afraid of my actors? Am I honest with them? Am I specific, or do I tend to be vague and general? Am I worried about being a nice guy and never really tell them what I think, such as, "Look, you're way off in that scene, and this is the way it should be." Do I think that they know more about acting than I do and that therefore things will come together for them, when I'm not sure they will?

9. Have I become fatalistic and find myself settling for things I don't want? Shouldn't I be open with the actors and tell them?

10. Things are going well, but I don't tell my actors. I think I should encourage them, otherwise, they're always in the dark.

PART FOUR

THE DIRECTOR AS STAGER

Groundplans and the factors governing their form and function.

The issue of "reality."

Visualizing the external and internal life of the play through blocking, composition, and picturization.

Staging the action.

The uses of counterpoint, mood, atmosphere, and tone.

Problems of directing on the open stage.

Staging "the concept."

CHAPTER EIGHT

GROUNDPLANS

This chapter was written with the collaboration of the designer, Rich Rose, who is professor of theatre at UCLA and cochair of the Theatre Department. He is the author of *Drafting Scenery for Theatre, Film, and TV, Autocad Onstage,* and *Drawing Scenery.*

WHAT IS A GROUNDPLAN?

The right groundplan is like having film in the camera. It enables you to take your pictures with freedom, ease, and flexibility. A good groundplan will help you get laughs if it's a comedy and help with the dynamics and impact you're after if it's a tragedy.

The groundplan is the vessel that contains your composition, picturization, your movement patterns, your choreography, and ebb and flow of the show. It's where your actors live. Consequently, it's where your action lives.

The groundplan is the geography you and the designer have put on the stage. If you are doing an interior, it's where you've put the walls, the doors, the windows; and how you've placed the furniture and the stairs and different levels of the house, if called for. An exterior is where you've made entrances, exits, and placed furniture, trees, rivers, cottages, or anything else that is literally "on the ground" and used in the action.

Groundplans used to be hard enough to come up with when there was only the proscenium stage. Now with open stages the problem is compounded because where you place furniture, for instance, has to be considered in terms of sight lines.

Externalizing Subtext

The groundplan and the setting of it also represent the physical embodiment of the subtext of the play and the world of the characters.

In terms of a floor plan, the set designer's job is two-fold: To assist the actors in revealing the basic nature of their character through an accurate portrayal of their world that is in keeping with the style of the writing and the production. For example, where would this particular character in this particular play place her couch? What kind of couch is it? How does it reflect her tastes, her class, her economic realities or pretensions? And do people sit on it, or is it a showpiece meant for company only?

The designer's other assignment is to help the director reveal to the audience the purpose of each character in the play. For example, Biff and Happy's room in *Death of a Salesman,* did they arrange the furniture and objects there? Any arrangement forces certain stage pictures, compositions, relationships, juxtapositions, and movement that could be instrumental in exposing or underscoring subtextual themes. It is very much like going into a person's home, looking around, and assessing the kind of life that goes on there and how revealing or how much is hidden about the people who live there.

Both the designer and the director, in their separate ways, block the show in their mind by imagining the actors moving through the floor plan. Yes, there are issues such as how the physical world being creating reflects the internal life of the play, but there are practicalities to consider as well. Can the character say her line and get to the part of the set she needs to be next? This is done by imagining the stage pictures that will be created as a result of the design. You don't want the actor to deliver a crucial line up-left, for example, when the focus of the composition, due to an ill-conceived floor plan, places the focus down-right at that moment in the play.

There are some secondary influences that might also affect the placement of furniture and other elements on the ground plan: moving scenery and author's notes. If the set has scene changes, the positions of elements on the floor plan are often a compromise between ideal placement and the need to get things moving smoothly. When multiple settings are involved, the groundplan becomes a real challenge.

The Author's Stage Directions

Author's notes are an interesting issue. Sometimes you long for more than the sentence or two that has been given. Other authors are so explicit they seem to want to dictate the direction of the play by remote control through an overabundance of detail. However, following these kinds of specific directions, literally, is often futile. The directions the author gives is for another theatre and under different circumstances. Sometimes these directions travel to our own time, but more often the director and designer are better off if they create a shared vision that illuminates the play through their own responses. Ibsen may be very explicit about the details of the rooms his characters inhabit, but if the director and designer see the furniture placed on a frozen ice pond, who's to say their images won't be as effective today as Ibsen's original intentions were over a hundred years ago.

The intent of the groundplan is not to sabotage the author's meaning. It is to create a theatrical dynamic for it. Having studied the play, the designer and director begin to visualize parts of it and have a sense of what the staging should be. For example, if you see something very sweeping and lyrical, you won't see much furniture on the stage that will make an obstacle course for the actors. If, however, you do see an obstacle course with actors tumbling all over the stage, clutter will help you.

Proscenium Groundplans

When Tyrone Guthrie and his designer Tanya Moiseiwitsch developed the open stage as the Stratford, Ontario model, which was later adapted to the Guthrie Theatre version in Minneapolis, they envisioned a modern equivalent of the Elizabethan stage, complete with an inner-below and inner-above with the audience wrapped around three sides. It was a stage meant mainly for the classics: pageantry, spectacle, trumpets and drums, lyrical language, and economy of scenery. A play of Molière's could be done and all that was necessary on stage for the audience to know where they were was one needle point chair from the period of Louis XIV and a chandelier overhead. The design emphasis was put into costumes. Other pieces of furniture might have been brought out, but the ground plan was minimal in order to allow the play to breathe its full, larger-than-life existence. The attempt was to strip away the naturalistic clutter and the influence of the cinema.

A single chair placed in the center of a proscenium stage, on the other hand, might not be as effective unless you can break down that objectifying proscenium arch. (See next page.) Designers have used drapery to disguise the proscenium. They have used scenic panels in the style and mode of the setting and production to bring the audience into the visual world of the play. Designers, as well, have literally brought the world of the play out into the audience by putting the majority of the scenic elements and the action onto the apron downstage of the proscenium.

In this format the play is brought closer to the audience in a style and life free of the usual picture-frame restrictions of the proscenium. The key here is to not limit your imagination with old conventions and traditions, but to see the entire volume of space that is the stage you're working on, proscenium or not, as up for grabs. It's all there to be reinvented to suit your vision.

How Do I Make a Good Groundplan?

Students are always asking the above question and immediately answering it with, "I'll have the designer do that, won't I?" Taking the latter first, in school you won't always have a designer attached to your project. If you do, the groundplan is derived from a design/director collaboration with the director, knowing how he wants to stage the play, often taking the lead. The "How do I?" question is not so easy to answer because it's done through much trial and error.

If you have a model of the set, you can move the scenic elements around very easily—a door up-left, a window in the center, the piano stage left. If you don't have a model, you can make sketches. It's best if you can use rehearsal room or the stage, and with folding chairs map out the most effective positions of these scenic elements. Walk through the set yourself. Have your stage managers walk around. See what it feels like, how any of this is conforming to the images you had in your mind about the play, or how new images are inspired from it. What doesn't feel right, isn't right. Move the window unit, change the placement of the armchair. Hopefully, you will have walked through

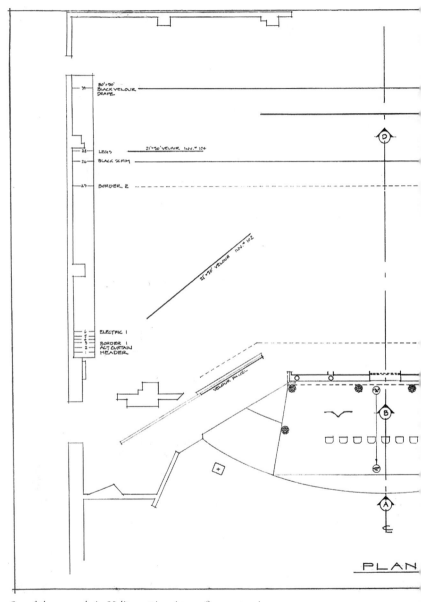

One of those one-chair-Molière settings in a modern proscenium
theatre—and I would like to think it worked.

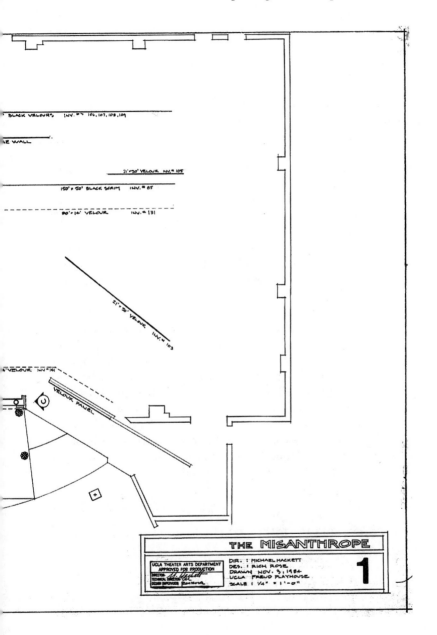

BLACK VELOUR'S   INV. #'S 106, 107, 108, 109

E WALL

21'×30' VELOUR INV.# 108'

150' × 50' BLACK SCRIM   INV.# 85

90' × 16' VELOUR   INV.# 131

21'× 30' VELOUR INV.# 103

4"VELOUR INV.#141

VELOUR PANEL

THE MISANTHROPE

UCLA THEATER ARTS DEPARTMENT
APPROVED FOR PRODUCTION
DIRECTOR.
TECHNICAL DIRECTOR
DESIGN SUPERVISOR.

DIR. : MICHAEL HACKETT
DES. : RICH ROSE.
DRAWN NOV. 3, 1984
UCLA FREUD PLAYHOUSE.
SCALE : 1/4" = 1'-0"

1

enough possibilities that you won't have to do much fussing and changing in rehearsals.

When Do I Commit?

Normally the groundplan has been set in almost-dry cement by the time of the first rehearsal. If problems are caught early enough it is easy to accommodate minor changes. Much later in the rehearsal process, it is more difficult and can even be expensive to make changes if they involve lighting—even impossible if they involve major scenic elements. Let's say we are close to opening and some lights have been hung and focused for a special scene on that couch upstage right. Moving the couch to center stage would mean that a crew would have to be called to reposition, recircuit, and refocus the lighting instruments. All the cues would then probably need to be rewritten into the lighting control board in order to eliminate the old circuit or dimmer instructions and include the new instrument instructions where appropriate.

Moreover, once you start blocking, you don't have the time to undo it all with a brand new idea such as, "I think we'll move the piano to the opposite side of the room, the sofa over there, and the fireplace downstage more." Some directors like to preblock a show without the actors, all the more reason to have worked out the groundplan. At this point, one can hear the question, "Is it better to preblock a show or work it out with the actors in rehearsal?" Before we get into the complexities of that, let's stick with groundplans.

There is no fortune cookie with the answer to groundplans on it. It's a puzzle whose solution depends on two things: 1) the nature of the particular play, and 2) the director's and designer's vision of how that play will be staged.

FACTORS THAT DETERMINE A GROUNDPLAN

A General Interest in Design

To a certain extent, directing is design, and, conversely, design is directing.

The director and designer attempt to find a physical shape to express the inner content of a play. Part of this process involves starting with the specific location(s) of the action of the play. *The Odd Couple* is written in a very real way. The set will most likely evoke a realistic apartment. On the other hand, the absurd writing style of Ionesco in *The Bald Soprano* will bend the reality of the scenic location to an extremely absurd design solution.

You are selecting what the audience is going to see in a very organized, esthetically-pleasing way. You are working with images, using actors to make pictures, compositions, and rhythms that are comprehensible on a literal or subconscious level. Therefore, directing students must take as many design and art history classes as they can, read as many books as possible on design, and become familiar with paintings, photographs, and museums. A foundation in design builds better directing bones. Actually, it builds better eyes. Design is the way the audience gets to see what the director and author see. In a film most of the audience is not aware how every shot was designed in tremendous detail. The lighting, the framing, the placement of the actors, the use of texture and color, and cinematography have all been labored over. Nothing is random. On stage, the same things occur; the director and designer's eyes replace the camera.

A Sense of Time and Place

The objects and their arrangement on the stage will convey many things. Put a throne on a bare stage and the audience knows the locale. Put a hammock between two trees and we have a different feeling. We are reminded of a country, of leisure, of summer, of something pleasant. Thus, the scenic elements that are part of your groundplan can have particular connotations for the audience. However, you might be dealing with material that is consciously not familiar to the audience. Its desire is to create a world no one has ever seen or known before.

Take this setting for example, "Bare interior. Gray light. Left and right back, high up, two small windows, curtains drawn. Front right, a door. Hanging near door, its face to wall, a picture. Front left, touching each other, covered with an old sheet, two ash bins. Center, an armchair on casters, covered with an old sheet . . ."

That's Beckett's description of the setting for *Endgame*, a world, if you can call it that, encapsulated inside its own isolation that has no bearing to much we're familiar with. The ash bins are recognizable, as well as the armchair and the ladder one of the characters is standing on. What we see is very disorienting. We don't know where we are. It's a mystery. Instead of the play flying out of the room in its own amorphousness, however, it is grounded in those recognizable objects.

In a Shakespeare play, if the army is bivouacked on a field, a dozen tents aren't necessary for the audience to know where they are. One tent will say it for them. As for the time of day, a lantern will say it's night. A trumpet says it's reveille and the over-used cry of the cock will announce morning.

The point is that the audience does not need a whole lot of scenic elements inside the groundplan to anchor it in time and place.

Sight Lines

Sometimes you'll see scenes with the sofa in front of the door, a large table in front of the sofa, and an end table blocking another door. When the curtain goes up, you don't know if you're witnessing an apartment that's been ransacked or if the messy placement of the furniture is the work of a very careless director. Sight lines refer to the view the audience has of the action. If you block their view, you are limiting their ability to see all the action. It's very important the director has a groundplan that keeps the action visible for all members of the audience. Sometimes, as a member of the audience, you can sit on the side of the orchestra or balcony and miss key events that were staged out of your view. This should never be the case. Equally destructive to sight lines are objects or scenic elements that mask pivotal action. This happens in the open stage when a customer's seat is right behind a huge chest of drawers which he can barely see over. Instead of witnessing the play he feels like he's hiding on the set waiting to be discovered.

These things in the way are not only visual barriers but psychological barriers as well. Even a six-foot-high fence in front of the scene places a psychological wall between the audience and the actor.

Platforms, as well, can cause the same kind of problems. If the platform is too high, the actor's feet can be hidden by the front of the platform. Here, again, is an obstacle that the director and the designer have placed between the actor and the audience. These aren't impossible obstacles to overcome, but solutions often involve the performer making the contact with the audience that the design and direction have failed to.

Variety

The lone chair in the Molière play has great impact, but may soon become tiresome. Other chairs are needed and brought on as the play progresses. The one chair is fine for a monologue or a few twosome scenes, but once the ensemble enters, answering such questions as the following becomes difficult: Where are they to sit? Or are they all to stand? Do they stand in a lump, or can they be arranged in interesting ways? The groundplan has to be flexible enough to give you the variety and versatility you envision in your staging, which demands a variety of placement for actors, a variety of movement patterns, and a variety of entrances and exits.

What about a play which is monochromatic and singular in tone such as Beckett's *Endgame*? Fortunately, that claustrophobic world is occasionally relieved by the fact Hamm's chair is on coasters and can be moved, as well as Clov's ladder, thereby making an ever-changing groundplan. It's almost as though Beckett knows when the play has run out of oxygen and demands another infusion.

Taking a closer look at Jo Mielziner's famous set for Arthur Miller's *Death of a Salesman* shows a great variety of playing areas. The house itself contains a kitchen, a fragment of Willy and Linda's bedroom, and, above, the bedroom of Biff and Happy. There are places surrounding the house that designate the outside world and are used for other interiors. The play is segmented into memories and lends itself to a multiplicity of playing areas.

Groups or isolated figures can be arranged in sections of the stage. Some on levels, some on the above, and some on furniture variously placed on stage.

On the other hand, today's audiences might have some trouble with the Mielziner designer. Today's television watching audience is used to close-up shots and reaction shots. That upper bedroom in *Salesman* was up a full two stories. Now just try and combine the double psychological barriers of height and distance with audiences used to more immediacy in their psychological drama. You have a scenic method that has difficulty working today.

In order to remedy this problem, the designer can attack both issues—height and distance. Bring the floor plan as far downstage as possible. Don't hesitate to break the proscenium or curtain line. The second-story bedrooms will need to be upstage of the lower-floor rooms. By getting everything downstage as much as possible, you are reducing the physical distance of the second-story rooms.

The second issue is height. You can raise second-story rooms by only a token amount—three to four feet. Audiences don't need the physical reality of a real seven-foot-high second story. By prominently including a staircase to reinforce the idea of going upstairs, this suggestion of height is enough to give the sense of an upstairs. Even though it is not a full seven feet, this height can provide enough physical separation for a sense of an upstairs space.

It's not necessary to throw out the idea of using different levels. Those scenes really do play better at a different elevation. Even if the height difference in minimal, the illusion of isolation will be furthered by the right lighting, focused carefully and colored differently than that used in the rest of the house. What you might lose in believable height is more than made up for in gaining a more intimate audience/actor relationship.

Focus

Directing is largely the ways you place ideas and characters in focus. We'll discuss this further when we get to staging, but even without actors on the set, the groundplan should help the audience know where to look. If you recall the exercise where we staged the dozen highlights of a story, you might want to look at the entire play that way. What are the dozen or so high moments and how do you see them? Your groundplan should help you achieve what you're visualizing. When evolving the original staging of John Guare's *The House of Blue Leaves*, the piano was all over the model. Finally, the obvious hit the director and the designer. The piano belonged upstage center, because it represented all the protagonists dreams and aspirations—and because the entire play was his audition to get to Hollywood. The piano was also placed in front of a window unit with bars that suggested a kind of imprisonment one felt in this environment, and how important it was to get out. The furniture below the piano was raked at angles that augmented focus onto the piano.

In comedy, farce in particular, doors are pivotal to laughter. A funny entrance or a great exit must be carefully conceived in terms of focus. There is no formula for this, but there are several things to consider:

1. An entrance area that plays a very important part in the play might be raised at least one level. This way the actor making the entrance has some height over the rest of the people in the room. The entrance is focused, almost underlined, because of the height.

2. If there are a number of exits with very funny lines that will get big laughs, keep that area in the clear. In other words, the actor should not be behind a table or sofa, masking half his body as he goes out the door with the funny line. Body language is as important as verbal jokes in a comedy.

3. Coming in and out, just missing each other by seconds, hiding—all are part of the rhythm of comedy. This means once a flow of action has been built, it has to be kept up. A flight of stairs with doors on an upper balcony is classic farce action. Going up and down the stairs can be funny. But how many stairs to that flight? Too many and the laugh has been lost. Once that happens, interest with that character has been lost, and the audience is seeking entertainment elsewhere on the stage.

Focus doesn't mean you have to underline what you want the audience to look at with red paint. Focus during a play often changes, but when you go over the dozen visual high points in your mind, you're going to see parts of the groundplan being more dominant than others. Those parts are what you need to give emphasis to.

Movement of the actors, as well, is another tool to help create balance, focus, harmony, and tension. The axis of the floor plan has strong influence over the movement of the actors. Theoretically, actor movement that is parallel—and perpendicular—to the main axis of the performance space is nonthreatening and gives a sense of harmony and well-being. (See page 138.) Movement that is diagonal to the space and the proscenium is more dynamic and evokes dramatic tension. (See page 140.) Designing the scenic elements, whether it be a house or a nowhere, along the appropriate axis—and therefore influencing the movement of the actors—is a powerful tool with strong implications for affecting the audience's emotional reaction to the play.

Balance

Often a student director will set up a scene and the groundplan gives the impression of falling off one end of the stage. If the door is stage left, the couch stage left, the coffee table stage left, the television set stage left with all the action taking place stage left, it ought to occur to the director to put something on the opposite side of the stage to balance it. Balance keeps the eyes of the audience limited to what you want it to see. If the groundplan is unbalanced, the viewers will tend to look past the frame you've intended for them. If everything is falling off one side of the stage, say into the back end of the theatre and out to the west side of the block, that's where the audience's eyes will go. If the stage is balanced, their eyes are always kept inside the limits of the stage.

However, you don't want to confuse balance with symmetry, which is common in beginning set designers. It's important to realize that the director and designers have the capacity to ignite a play or diffuse its power through their use or misuse of balance, composition, and focus.

Balance is always important—required in fact. A balanced composition allows you as director to control the focus. An out-of-balance composition will never let you get a handle on the focus.

Symmetry, on the other hand, is an option in a balanced composition. Balancing a composition doesn't require symmetry, however. Symmetry can be a good choice in certain kinds of plays, where appropriate—usually works that are quite stylized. These are typically plays whose core ideas are about symmetry. Symmetry is harmony. Most often these are classic and neoclassic verse plays, as well as the plays of Molière and Restoration comedy. In these plays, symmetry represents balance, balance is order, our emotions are ruled by our intellect, and nothing is in excess. The paradox is what is going on underneath these ordered, perfect universes is forbidden love, lust, murder, revenge, betrayal, madness, hypocrisy, and all that mankind has done or will do.

In psychological drama, symmetry is rarely a solution. Society no longer requires the form of an ordered world imposed on us by the gods or kings. But the absence of symmetry requires greater invention to create visual balance to tell our very different stories.

FREQUENTLY ASKED QUESTIONS

Q: I know exactly the groundplan I want. Do I give it to the designer and let her work from there, or do I wait until she comes up with her own plan?

A: Either way. She might be helped by the way you see it.

Q: I've recently had a bad experience where the designer gave me a set I did not want. How do I avoid that again?

A: "Gave" you! She shouldn't be giving you the set and you shouldn't be giving her the design. You have to take the time to build a collaboration which evolves into a mutually agreed upon approach to the play.

Q: But sometimes people have conflicting aesthetics. I prefer a minimalist approach . . . that one chair image you spoke of. I'm always ending up with these ornamental and Baroque designers. Something is always compromised. I don't want a door center, and it's put center, that sort of thing. What do I do?

A: We're straying from groundplans and going into two other areas—the issue of collaboration and the issue of compromise. But perhaps it's all interlocked.

All I can say is that compromise should result as something you've gained, nothing that's been lost. Compromise should mean you've given up an idea, but got a better one in return. The other person's way of doing something was "righter." But if a solution does not propel your thinking in that "righter" direction, you shouldn't use it.

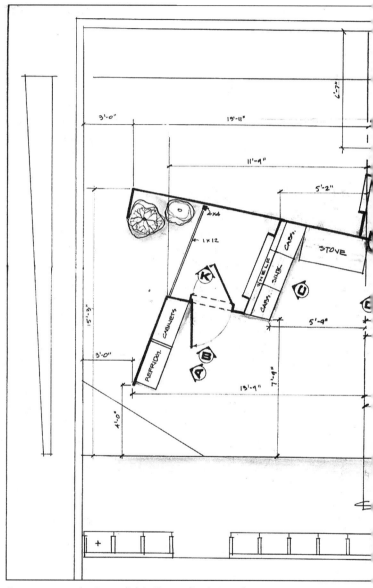

Actor movement that is parallel (and perpendicular) to the main axis of the performance space is nonthreatening, and reeks

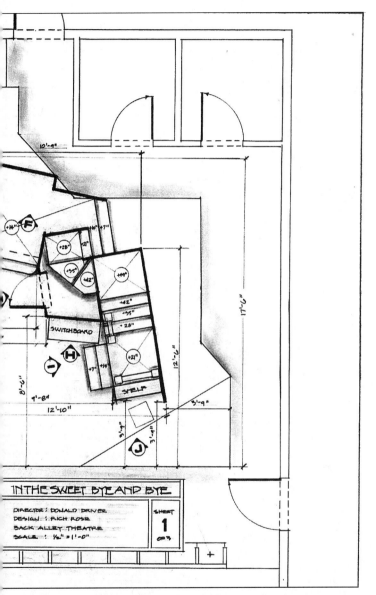

of harmony and well-being.

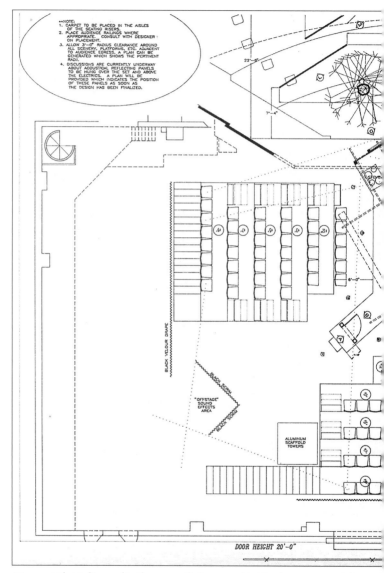

Movement that is diagonal to the space and the proscenium that is more dynamic and evokes dramatic tension.

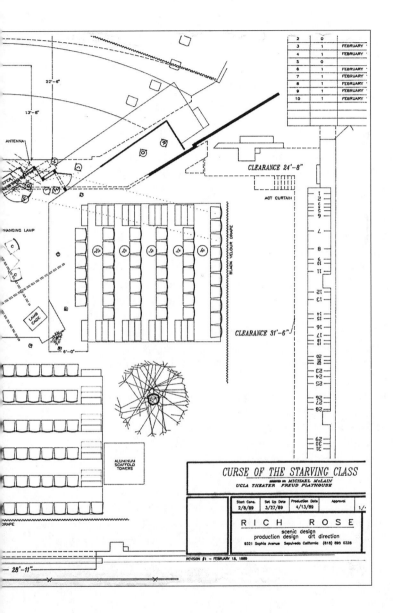

CURSE OF THE STARVING CLASS
DIRECTED BY MICHAEL McLAIN
UCLA THEATER   FREUD PLAYHOUSE

	Start Cons.	Set Up Date	Production Date	Approval	
	2/8/89	3/27/89	4/13/89		1/.

R I C H   R O S E
scenic design
production design   art direction
9321 Sophia Avenue   Sepulveda California   (818) 893 0328

Q: Do you always do a mock-up of the set?

A: In the rehearsal room or on the model, yes. I have to see if the groundplan has:

Variety

Balance

Focus

A sense of place

I have to feel the images I have in my head will play on the groundplan. The designer is always with me, because we need each other's help.

Q: Haven't you ever wanted a new set in the middle of rehearsal? Haven't you realized you made a mistake and need to make drastic changes?

A: Yes. But the choices aren't pretty. If I change groundplans I have to reblock the play. I also have to let the designer and producer know about the changes, which may affect the budget. It also means all I'm doing is rehearsing my staging and not rehearsing the actors and the play. If changes mean minor adjustments and can be executed with very little waste of time, sure, go for it.

Q: But what if the play isn't working and it's more than a minor adjustment?

A: It's common, especially in the commercial theatre, when the show isn't working to do the following:

a) Throw out the set.

b) Get new costumes.

c) Fire some of the actors.

d) Fire the director.

e) Rewrite the script.

It's unfortunate that the set is the first thing to be blamed. It's also unfortunate the producers will eventually get to ∂, fire the director. If the play isn't working, it may very well be that you're groundplan is wrong and nothing can be staged on it. It may also be perfectly right, but you aren't telling the story on it very well.

That is why your preparations with the designer and exploration of the groundplan before rehearsals is so important.

CHAPTER NINE

STAGING

Everything you put onto the stage — scenery, costumes, lights, performances — is part of staging the show. Staging also includes:

Blocking.

Picturizing.

Composition.

Counterpoint.

Enhancements to staging include:

Tone.

Mood.

Atmosphere.

There is also the issue of staging one way for the proscenium stage and another way for the round, three-quarter, or any type of "open stage."

However, before going on to discuss the specifics of staging, one has to decide what reality one is creating. If there is one thing that the director is completely in control of, it's the reality that the show is going to be playing in. When you are working through blocking, evolving picturization and images, expressing ideas through visual compositions, you are placing the audience into a very particular world, a very particular reality.

The Issue of Reality

For example, blocking can be psychologically motivated or very stylized, depending on what look you want the play to have. That look is based on the reality that you're working in. You might want everything to seem natural, as though these were events that were happening to real people. In that case, the blocking has to appear to be motivated. A character goes to the window, not arbitrarily, but for a specific reason. Notice that I said, "the blocking has to appear . . ." This is because no blocking is ever completely motivated by character needs. Sometimes stage practicalities take over from psychology. If one character is standing in front of another, one of the actors should move over. If a move would heighten the focus of a stage picture, you make the move and fill in the psychology later. If a scene has been playing too long in one place, you will want to block in moves to give it variety. If it's psychologically valid for an actor be in a place that does not afford the best sight lines, you have to adjust the actor for the sake of the audience. None of this is to discredit psychological motivation, need, or reason as long as they are part of a somewhat larger truth: stageworthiness.

George Abbott, the legendary Broadway director, asked an actor to move stage right. The actor said, "What's my motivation?" Mr. Abbott replied, "Your paycheck!" You can imagine that the actor, who didn't want to lose his job, quickly found his character's motivation for moving stage right.

If you're working on a scene and find everyone clumped in a certain spot and need to have an actor be on the opposite side of the stage to balance the picture, it's not unseemly to ask the actor, "Would you move over there on such and such a line? I need the stage balanced." The actor will usually oblige, finding his motivation later. It's like knowing where the light is. If the actor has the choice between being "real" or being visible, he will certainly choose to find the hot spot first. He knows that there's no sense in being "real" in the dark. Obviously, he's not going to let the audience know that he's moved over to be in the light. The move will be fully "justified" and seem perfectly right after he fills it in.

If you're working in a heightened reality or a very stylized piece your staging does not have to conform to conventional notions of motivation. You and the actors will invent your own world with its own logic. Look at musicals. Characters can be talking quite naturally, then suddenly go into a ballet or song at the drop of a hat. Their dancing or singing is a metaphor for their feelings, their relationships, their dreams. The movement is nonliteral and not necessarily motivated but rather evolves out of its own drama and aesthetic. In *commedia dell'arte*, the actors wear masks. Movement springs from another set of conventions: stock characters who represent certain types. The *doctore*, for example, is unlike any person we've ever seen, yet he's a parody of every medical quack we've ever known. *Commedia* is not about everyday. It's about universals. It's the distilled essence of what we know made ridiculous. It goes to the most fantastic lengths to externalize the inner comedy that lives in all of us.

Albert Camus once defined style as "what we accept or reject from reality." The more we accept, the less stylized a piece is. The less we accept, the more stylized.

I once saw an American director's "Kabuki" version of *Woyzzeck*, which was staged like a Japanese theatre piece, moves, gestures, costumes and all. The production worked except when the lines were spoken. Real words and ritualized movement were at stark variance with each other. As an audience member I felt that what I was seeing had nothing to do with what I was hearing. The director would have been better off had he ritualized the text as well. You can't really work in two realities at the same time. Determine which reality you are in and take each as far as it will go.

BLOCKING

Blocking refers to the moves of the actors. Terms such as *cross downright, move up-left, sit on the sofa,* and *cross to the bar and mix the drink* are examples of blocking. The term *blocking* itself always make me think of something that is temporary. Artists blocked out their canvases, then painted over the blocking. In the early stages of blocking, it is a sketch to be filled in eventually or altered. After blocking is "set" or "frozen," it is where the actor goes every performance.

There are many approaches to blocking. Here are some:

- The director has preblocked the play in his script, and as the actors rehearse, he tells them where to move, based on his plan.
- The director is very spontaneous about the blocking and works it out as the play unfolds in rehearsals.
- The director lets the actors decide where and when they want to move. When the actors are satisfied, the director is satisfied, and that becomes the blocking.
- Everyone agrees that blocking is arbitrary and should change with however one feels each night of the show. Hence, the blocking is always different, depending on the actors' inspiration during the performance.

If the latter two examples work for you, and it's the kind of work you're into, go for it.

And if preblocking helps you, I suggest that that is the way you should work. The problem with preblocking a show is that it leaves out a major given: the actor. It assumes that the director will make the best choices from her private rationale. It leaves out what the actor can and will bring to the occasion. I think some scenes, such as large ensemble scenes, must be worked out in advance. But watch out—there's a trap. You may tend to look at the scene only in terms of how you figured it out in your living room and be oblivious to how it's living on the stage.

I prefer to find the blocking in rehearsal with the actors for several reasons. First, my eye follows my ear. What I mean by this is that as I hear the line I get the message how it should move. Everything I do in rehearsal comes from the way I'm hearing the text.

Second, I need to sense where I can take each actor. I don't know until the actor is in rehearsal where his intuitions really lie. After I find out, I can help the actor bring out what's inside of him. I may feel that the actor has something going on inside that would reveal an aspect of his character in a very special way if he makes a certain move or does a particular piece of business. For instance, I might suggest, "How about standing on your head when you cross to the fireplace." I'd never suggest this if I didn't have a hunch that the actor can accept such a direction. I also have to know, if he's crazy enough to try it, that he's going to look good doing it; if I think he won't, I won't suggest it. At other times, you might have an idea for a piece of staging but feel that it should be something the actor himself has to come to. Maybe one day he'll come up and say, "I have an idea. What if I stand on my head when I'm at the fireplace?"

When you're blocking, many questions run through your mind:

1. Is the move motivated?   As we've discussed, the move should *seem* to be motivated. The next question is, "What motivates a move?" I'm frightened by what's outside the door, so I move away from it. On the other hand, I may be frightened but also compelled to find out what is going on. In that case, I open the door. In the second instance, I added an action: "to find out what's going on."

Moves are motivated by actions. It's only when the director gives a move that is contrary to the character's action that she and the actor

will tangle over it. Another term for *action* is *beat*. You'll hear a director in rehearsal say, "On the next beat cross to the bed." Or, "On the
beat before you hit him, move closer to the table," and so forth. What
the director is talking about is the specific action that the actor is
playing at that moment. When there is a major change of action or
"beat," either you or the actor will hopefully find a need to illuminate
it through the blocking. Romeo can be in the garden wooing Juliet
from a distance, but comes the time when the actor will have an
impulse to attempt a climb up the walls to her balcony. This impulse
comes from what he has heard Juliet say to him—something so
provocative that he can restrain himself no longer. Remember that
just as the director has to keep listening to the text, so does the actor.
All impulses derive from listening onstage. If your actors are compelled to stay where they are, letting whole events, recognitions,
reversals, and turning points fly by, remaining static and glued to the
spot, it's because they are not listening, and neither are you.

2. Is the actor helped by the blocking?   Remember that the actor
has to find the logic and purpose behind everything he's saying and
doing. He's got to find his own foundation for playing the role. And
you have to help him and not lie back and wait for the actor to come
up with interesting staging and perfect pieces of business. (He
shouldn't have to do both the acting and directing at the same time.)
Essentially the blocking that is created liberates the character. The
character is freed from the actor's imagination after it's able to take
flight onstage. You help the character move where it wants to go; and
you help it by restraining it at other times.

If you find that the blocking is not helping the actor, there's no
sense in blaming the actor for not being able to fulfill your brilliance.
You have to change the blocking until you find what works for both
of you. It's been my experience that new adjustments usually take
about three rehearsals before they work. Give the actor time to allow
the move or business to become second nature. You have to learn the
difference between something that doesn't work, something that
won't ever work, and something that will, in time, work.

3. Does the blocking illuminate what the scene is about?   Does your
staging tell the story? For example, the second act of *Hedda Gabler*

opens with a scene between Hedda and Judge Brack. It takes place in her drawing room. She's bored, restless, and feeling trapped within a new marriage. She confesses her feelings to her old friend, Judge Brack. He uses the information to offer her a way out of her unexciting life: have an affair with him. Ibsen wrote it as a "sit-down scene." Brack is in one chair, Hedda is in the other, and page after page of dialogue goes on. You might find that the suggested stillness works very well. But it might not. How heavily does Judge Brack pursue what he's after? How subtle is he? Hedda doesn't seem to pick up on his suggestion. Is she naive, or is she avoiding his implications? The scene is about how one exploits the misfortune of others for one's own self-interest. Brack is a predator, and this is one of the few times that we see Hedda as a vulnerable woman.

She can go to a window when she's restless and have her back to the Judge when he makes his offer for a "triangular relationship," which would have less of an impact on her. She might make the two of them drinks because she wants something to do, or she might play with her pistols, which have been part of the scene.

You can open the scene up for improvisational investigation:

You might stage the scene with the image of a trapped animal (Hedda) and a sympathetic onlooker (Judge Brack) who wants to free her.

You could try prefacing each line with "I want" and let the actors move wherever their "I want"s take them. This may help you to discover a great many new impulses from the actors. After Hedda's inner turmoil and Brack's lust come out and are part of the characters' inner fiber, you may very well want to stage the scene very simply. The subtext is there, seething underneath the action. Now, if the actors are just sitting, quietly playing the scene, it can be powerful because so much is going on within them and between them.

4. Am I *sustaining dramatic tension?*   If the characters are static without a strong inner life, the scene will have no energy. If the scene has too much movement the story will become diffuse. After Judge Brack insinuates that he should become Hedda's lover, the air should be filled with tension. How will she react? But she seems to be oblivious to the suggestion. He pursues it rather obliquely several more times. The tension builds. Is there stillness between them, or does he circle her quietly like an animal playing with its prey? Which is more powerful? The problem is that you don't know until you've tried it both ways. Take every opportunity to explore as many approaches in blocking the tension of a scene as possible because the actors will play every approach differently. Every move will suggest another way of playing their action. Instead of being direct about something, a move can help the actor be indirect, subtle, tossing off the big suggestion. The judge might just sit at a table and peel an apple, never looking at Hedda. It depends on what you want. I always think of blocking as being in an editing room. Every time I restage the scene, I have another choice of how it will read to the audience.

5. *Is the character's behavior being revealed accurately?* If you looked at just one character through the course of a play and observed how he moves, what his body is like in repose, the activities that he indulges in, such as reading a newspaper, eating, drinking, working, chasing the opposite sex around the room, fistfighting, you would have a pretty clear idea who and what he is. On the other hand, what you and the actor choose to hold back can be equally illuminating. If the character desires something very strongly but makes no move toward it, if he represses his need and behaves in a contradictory way, it can be equally eloquent. I always think it's healthy for the actor and director to try out many ideas, even ones that are way out. There should be no air of, "He wouldn't do this or wouldn't do that" about the rehearsal process. How does anyone know what the character would or wouldn't do until it's tried? Actors will usually do anything (at least once) for their director, and directors have to reciprocate.

Staging the "Action"

If you block your show not only in terms of what the script physically obliges you to do, such as "cross to the samovar and serve the officers tea," but also in terms of giving moves according to the characters' change of actions or "beats," you will find your staging to be motivated, have variety, and be rhythmically varied. The actions are the ever-changing tactics or strategies that each character is attempting in order to get what he or she wants. They're what makes the character interesting.

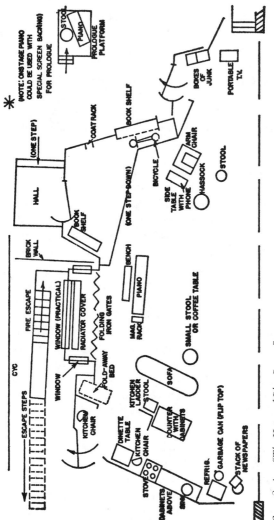

Scene design: "The House of Blue Leaves"

Let's put some of the principles that have been discussed into an example by staging a section of a scene. I've chosen the "cook for me" scene from John Guare's *The House of Blue Leaves* (see page 150).

First, the groundplan.

Notice how the furniture is moved from the walls, creating a number of playing areas: the kitchen, the sofa, the easy chair and TV, the piano, and the window with a practical fire escape. The groundplan, which has a very heavy amount of scenic elements in the kitchen area stage right, is balanced by the armchair down-left. The TV set, which is on casters, can move in front of the armchair or anywhere in that area, providing a variety of uses. The shape of the groundplan is almost triangular with the piano as the apex, creating a natural focus to the room. Upstage right you'll notice an alcove between the kitchen wall and the window. That's where Artie's foldaway bed is stored. When the play begins he is sleeping on it, center stage, parallel with the sofa. (His wife, Bananas, sleeps alone in their bedroom.) Artie is a zookeeper in Central Park and an amateur songwriter who just experienced being unappreciated at the El Dorado bar and grill amateur night. He is asleep inside his sleeping bag on his foldaway bed when his neighbor—who is also the woman he wants to run off to Hollywood with—Bunny Flingus bursts into the apartment, urging him to get downstairs to witness the pope's motorcade on Queens Boulevard. Bunny is convinced that the pope will bless Artie's music, which will make them rich and famous.

Bunny finally persuades Artie to get out of bed, saying, "It's not too late to start. With me behind you! Oh, Artie, the El Dorado Bar will stick up a huge neon sign flashing onto Queens Boulevard, in a couple of years flashing 'Artie Shaughnessy Got Started Here.' And nobody'll believe it. Oh, Artie, tables turn."

Artie: *(thoughtful, sings)*
Bridges are for burning,
Tables are for turning—

(He turns on all the lights. He pulls BUNNY by the pudgy arm over to the kitchen.) I'll go see the Pope—

Bunny: *(hugging him)* Oh, I love you!

Artie: I'll come if—

Bunny: You said you'll come. That is tantamount to a promise.

Artie: I will if—

Bunny: Tantamount. Tantamount. You hear that? I didn't work in a law office for nix. I could sue you for breach.

Artie: *(seductively)* Bunny?

Bunny: *(near tears)* I know what you're going to say—

Artie: *(opening a bottle of ketchup under her nose)* Cook for me?

Bunny: I knew it. I knew it.

Artie: Just breakfast.

Bunny: You bend my arm and twist my heart but I got to be strong.

Artie: I'm not asking for any ten-course dinner.

Bunny: Just put your clothes on over the ski p.j.'s I bought you. It's thirty-eight degrees and I don't want you getting your pneumonia back—

Artie: *(holding up two eggs)* Eggs, baby. Eggs right here.

Bunny: *(holding out his jingling trousers)* Rinse your mouth out to freshen up and come on let's go?

Artie: *(seductively)* You boil the eggs and pour lemon sauce over—

Bunny: Hollandaise, I know hollandaise. It's really cold out, so dress warm—Look, I stuffed the *New York Post* in my booties— plastic just ain't as warm as it used to be.

Artie: And you pour the hollandaise over the eggs on English muffins—and then you put the grilled ham on top—I'm making a scrapbook of all the foods you tell me you know how to cook and then I go through the magazines and cut out pictures of what it must look like. Look—veal parmagiana—eggplant meringue.

Bunny: I cooked that for me last night. I was so good I almost died.

Artie: *(sings)*

> If you cooked my words
> Like they was veal
> I'd say I love you
> For every meal.
> Take my words,
> Garlic and oil them,

Butter and broil them,
Sauté and boil them—
Bunny, let me eat you!

(speaks) Cook for me?

Bunny: Not till after we're married.
Artie: You couldn't give me a sample right now?
Bunny: I'm not that kind of girl.

The artist's conception of the set.

Bunny imagines it's her wedding day and she should have something white at her throat. This is truly a day of miracles.

Her action is to inspire Artie so she kneels down to hug him. "Oh, Artie, the El Dorado Bar will stick up a huge neon sign flashing onto Queens Boulevard, in a couple of years flashing 'Artie Shaugnessy Got Started Here.'"

Artie is convinced. He embraces her, showing that he shares her dream. Happy, he sings, "Bridges are for burning, tables are for turning."

But he's starved and pulls her into the kitchen to cook for him. She's this great cook who has never cooked anything for him. He proposes a bargain, "I'll come if . . ." She knows what's coming and her action is to avoid making any such deal. "You said you'll come. That is tantamount to a promise. . ."

He needs to lure her and opens a bottle of catsup like it's seductive perfume. "Cook for me?" Bunny's action is to be strong against this kind of temptation, "I knew it. I knew it."

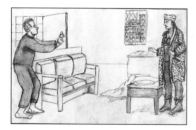

She runs out of the kitchen to the other side of the cot. She must resist, "You bend my arm and twist my heart, but I got to be strong." Artie comes down stage, holding two eggs and trying to show how little he's asking for, "I'm not asking for any ten-course dinner."

Bunny must hold steady and she does this by changing the subject. She grabs his trousers, "Just put your clothes on over the ski p.j.'s I bought you." Artie is persisting, showing her how simple it would all be, "Eggs, baby. Eggs right here."

He lures her by moving from down stage right to up center on the opposite side of the cot. She backs away, trying not to give in. Artie woos her like a lover with, "You boil the eggs and pour lemon sauce over . . ." Bunny is about to cave in, but she remembers her mission which is to get him out to see the Pope pass by. "It's really cold out so dress warm."

Artie cuddles to her with the eggs like they're diamonds, trying to seduce her, "And you pour the Hollandaise over the eggs on English muffins. . ."

All he can think about is her cooking. He runs to find a scrapbook that he falls asleep by, which is filled with pictures of meals. "I'm making a scrapbook of all the foods you tell me you know how to cook and then I go through the magazines and cut out the pictures of what it must look like." His action is to show her he's built a kind of shrine to her cooking.

As he gets the scrapbook and talks about it, Bunny walks from the kitchen to take a good look at it.

She takes the scrapbook and sits down to admire her own skills as what she can do. Her heart is broken and she remarks about how good this particular recipe is, "I cooked that for me last night. It was so good I almost died."

Artie senses she may break her resistance and tries to serenade her. He runs to the piano and improvises a tune:
"If you cooked my words
Like they was veal
I'd say I love you
For every meal. . ."

He races to the sofa and dances on it, trying to coax her, cheer her, charm her. "Cook for me."

She is holding firm with, "Not 'til after we're married." And he goes to his knees, begging, "You couldn't give me a sample right now?"

She will not be swayed and says, "I'm not that kind of girl." At which point he collapses on her lap in utter frustration.

PICTURIZATION AND COMPOSITION

As the director is blocking the scenes, other questions come to mind, such as, "Can I get this scene picturized better? Are these visual images telling the story?" And after the scene is blocked the director steps back, looks at it, and asks, "Is the stage composition I've put up there interesting to look at? Does it express the feeling I'm trying to get across?" Just as the painter tries to find the strongest images for her canvas and the cinematographer the most dynamic image for his camera, the director, who thinks very much the same, is trying to find the picture, the stage composition that "really does it" for each and every moment.

Picturization

Usually, if the scene works, it will be picturized correctly. If you have any doubts about whether or not the scene is working, check it visually. Turn off the sound and let the actors just go through the staging. If it appears random, disorganized, or clumsy, that's because it's playing that way. If it doesn't look right, it ain't right! On the other hand, a beautiful picture does not always mean that the scene is working, either. It may mean that it's just a nice picture that may or may not have anything to do with the scene.

The author picturizes by the use of images and stories. *Oedipus*, for example, is a cornucopia of images relayed to the audience by what the characters say they have seen. The pictures are literal, graphic, but often descriptive of emotional states and abstract ideas. There are events onstage that are also powerful visually, such as the entrance of Oedipus blinded. At its center, *Oedipus* is a play where truth is made visible through verbal and visual images. And not to be reductive, you might say that this dramatic revelation of one truth after the other is the center of drama itself.

Actors picturize. It's the way they manifest the essence of who they are playing. Characterization is really what the actor has chosen to both externalize and internalize his role. The actor is giving you an internal story by showing you motivations, actions, and feelings. He's giving you an external story by showing you movement, gestures, voice, and bearing.

Viewed this way, the director organizes the pictures in the text and those of her own invention in order to convey:

The emotional texture of the moment.   The stage picture will express what the characters are feeling, thereby conveying it to the audience. In the opening of John Guare's *The House of Blue Leaves*, a man is inside a sleeping bag as a woman fully dressed for a cold day circles around him, urging him to get out of his cocoon. The picture gives you a sense of one person pumping life into another. Because of the contrast between the characters, he in long johns, she dressed for the freezing cold with a camera and binoculars dangling from her neck, there is a sense that we are watching a comedy.

Relationships.   A picture can always express exactly where a relationship is at any given moment. As the situation changes, the relationship between characters often changes. There is a visual interplay between characters all the time. In the comedic picture of Artie and Bunny is Bananas, Artie's wife, who is privy to their plot of abandoning her. She is literally a part of the picture and won't be pushed out. She crawls around the floor, observing them until she decides to make an entrance, giving them plenty of warning for Bunny to leave. Instead, Bunny hides in the kitchen, and now the picture is reversed. Bunny is on all fours, overhearing Artie and his wife. These pictures are always comedic, but because Bananas is "sick," there is always an edge and sense of danger to the scenes she is in. The situation is of a triangular relationship, with Bunny trying to part Artie from Bananas.

The basic situation.   Is the cooking scene a seduction? Is it a negotiation? Is it simply a hungry man begging for food? Is it a woman who can't give away the best part of herself until she's married? If you look at the "cook for me" scene and boil it down to its simplest core, you will find what my old teacher called the "basic situation." The basic situation is often deceptively simple. In the case cited, the basic situation is a very hungry man who wants some breakfast. After I know that, I can begin to find a way of staging this section. On the other hand, you may say, "To hell with boiling everything down to a basic situation. I'm going to work intuitively, feeling my way through the text, and after my work is done, it will tell me what it's about. I don't have to tell *it* what it's about. It already knows."

That's fine. Just expect to restage the scene many times until you feel that you finally have hit the nail on the head: "Ah, that's the core of it!" And that's when you know that the basic situation is being told by the picture and that the picture is illuminating the basic situation.

Note: Actors are often helped by knowing the pictures that you want and will help you to achieve them. In a good actor/director collaboration the actor will sometimes say, "I'm over here. Is this the picture you want?" or you will say, "I know it's a little arbitrary right now, but if you cry two feet further downstage, you'll be in focus." As you're blocking the scene you are continually attuned to where your staging is taking you and what pictorial shape is being made. And if you had certain pictures in mind for specific moments, you have to engineer the blocking into them. Don't be afraid of doing this. I always like to "get that picture out of my system." I've seen it for so long that I don't know if it will work or not, but I have got to at least try it. I don't want to sit there on opening night seeing pictures that I wished I had put onto the stage.

Exercises

Go through your family album and the albums of friends. What story does each photo tell you?

Go to the museum often. Study paintings of different periods. There are many videos dedicated to specific artists and schools of painting. Whenever you are working on a scene or a play, see if a painting, drawing, or cartoon that you've absorbed inspires you.

Keep a scrapbook of photos from daily newspapers that have special impact upon you. You never know when you'll use one.

Study the films that you like from the perspective of what has been put into each frame, how it has been organized, and how it affects you.

Composition

Composition is the organized placement of actors, lighting, and design elements on the stage. It is how the stage looks at any given moment. Composition is the arrangement of everything inside the painting's frame. It unifies all of the elements: form, pattern, color, and light. On a subliminal level it gives the audience a sense of completion and artistic wholeness to what it is seeing.

As you walk through the galleries of a museum observing the paintings, pay particular attention to what you are looking at. Ask yourself the following questions:

- What are my eyes drawn to in this painting?
- How has the arrangement of objects or people affected how my eyes move from one place to the other?
- Why are my eyes kept in the painting? In other words, what are the elements that keep my eyes from wandering off the canvas at the corners?
- How does the use of light help what I'm focused on?
- What shapes do I see within the overall composition? Triangles, diagonals, semicircles, converging lines?
- Is a mood or atmosphere evoked by the composition?
- Is a story being told?

Composition can have interpretive possibilities. For example, walk into any workplace where people are taking a break, and you will notice a particular composition. Some people will be talking, some smoking, some having coffee, a few on the telephone or just hanging out. There is a particular arrangement that they have unconsciously chosen to put themselves into. The people didn't say, "Oh, let's compose ourselves into an interesting series of diagonal lines, semicircles, and triangles." The composition that they are in happened due to their circumstances.

Ask yourself the following questions:

1. Does the composition give you a sense of how people are feeling individually or as a group? How many people like or dislike or are indifferent to each other? What tension exists between any of them? How can you tell?
2. Can a composition help reveal individual agendas? Observe a party. If you could put any section of this party into a painting, which one would it be? Look around in all the areas that people are in. Notice the way they either do or don't relate to

each other. Body language is telling you each person's agenda. The scene that you choose will have its own unity and probably be interestingly staged because real-life compositions tend to be that way.

As is so often the case in any art, the opposite is often true. A composition can also have no interpretive possibilities. It may exist as an abstract nonliteral entity. It may be there for the sake of its own design. It may evoke feelings in you that you cannot describe but that are stirred within you nevertheless. Or it may exist as a series of symbols that are there to tantalize you into interpretation. Dreamscapes, especially in dance, are compelling to watch. Certain films are designed nonliterally. They are a world unto themselves, a reality that only the artists who created them share. The audiences are witnesses to an event that has no emotional connection for them or intellectual implications. Meaning cannot be discerned. These pieces work in terms of movement and music. Sometimes no music, just rhythm. The patterns that the dancers make, how they are sculpted in three-dimensional space, the use of light and sound come together to make a series of compositions that are fascinating but that do not tell a story and may or may not have a private meaning for those involved. What does the audience share in all this? A kind of beauty, I think. And sometimes that's more than enough.

Picturization and composition are among the great pleasures in directing. Not to be pretentious, they are what I sometimes think of as the "art part" of directing. They are how your imagination expresses itself most vividly in the production. I suggest that the student director take art history classes and/or read as much as possible on the technical side of painting, design, and sculpture. Kenneth Clark's *Looking at Pictures* is a good place to start. Comic books and cartoon work, in general, are often examples of first-rate composition. There you'll see how action is storyboarded so well that cartoonists are often used in preproduction of films to map out the shots. Which brings me to the place where you'll really get an appreciation and a desire to picturize and compose: movies.

Rent the following films and examine them for their visual construction:

Fred Zinneman's **High Noon.**   Shot after shot is built on converging lines, emulating a railroad track with a threat to the hero on the way. Sometimes freeze the frame and observe how each shot has been composed and how complete and unified the overall shot appears. Observe how one shot leads meaningfully into the next, building a tremendous amount of dramatic tension pictorially.

Orson Welles's **Macbeth** *and* **Othello.**   The compositions in these films are drawn from contrasts between light and dark and from very dense perspective. Each frame can be studied for hours. What's often most impressive in the compositions is how Welles ties in the architecture of the locale, whether it be a Moorish arch or huge rocks against a hostile-looking sea. The camera angle is often low, looking up at these larger-than-life characters. Welles loved diagonal lines that give the scenes a kind of menace and threat.

Federico Fellini's **8 1/2.**   Here the feeling is quite the opposite of Welles or Zinneman. The compositions are essentially romantic with flowing circles, semicircles of women surrounding the protagonist much of the time. Also, the comic and grotesque aspects of the film create their own special compositions, which are always very original and offer you pictures you've never seen before.

Obviously a play can't do what a film can. But pictorial invention can be as varied and as compelling onstage. The famous photographer Edward Weston has said, "Good composition is only the strongest way of seeing the subject. It cannot be taught, because like all creative effort, it is a matter of personal growth." But it can be learned, mainly by looking, questioning, and experimenting yourself. My advice is:

> Go through the archives of former productions for photographs, not necessarily of plays you are working on, but of how other directors have used the stage.

> Get acquainted with the variety of scene design and how the best designers in the world have worked.

> Spend time in museums, just browsing around, before going into production.

Of course, you want to see as much theatre as possible, but don't limit yourself to plays and musicals. Go to the ballet or modern dance concerts to experience a larger visual vocabulary.

If it's in a theatre, go to it. If it's not in a theatre, but it's a theatrical event, be there: parades, festivals, street fairs, sidewalk performers, pageants.

You have to turn yourself into a lifelong student of staging.

FREQUENTLY ASKED QUESTIONS

Q: I'm directing my show, and the actor is not receptive to my blocking. When I give him the move he says, "I can't do that now" or "It's not the way I'm feeling" or "I have a better idea. How about such and such?"
What do I do?

A: Well, what have you been doing when the actor responds this way to your directions?

Q: I leave him alone. Sometimes when he says he has a better idea, it's okay but not what I wanted. But you talked about collaboration, so I feel I have to let him work out his process.

A: How's your show looking so far?

Q: I'm not too happy with it.

A: You know, there's a difference between collaborating and tyrannizing. Actor's tyranny is no better than director's tyranny. I think you have to have a firmer hand in rehearsals regarding your staging. If your actor was in a dance number, he wouldn't tell the choreographer what he would and wouldn't do. He'd have to execute the steps. It's the same with blocking. You can't leave it to the actor to stage himself for a number of reasons:

1. Very few are capable of it.
2. Most actors enjoy the help that creative blocking gives them.
3. The director is out front, observing, and is the best judge of how things are looking.
4. As the director you are in charge of the rhythm, dynamics, and flow of the play, which good blocking enhances.

Q: So I tell him to move when and where I think he should?

A: Absolutely. It is the actor's job to give the director what he or she wants. You can try it your way, you can try it his way. But you make the final selection. But you can't let things sit there, having tried nobody's way. I'll bet the show is very static and talky right now.

Q: It is.

A: Get in there and do your work and stop being intimidated by the actor.

Q: I have a question about picturization and composition. I recently saw a musical and was very impressed by the staging. The director's use of pictures and the way he composed everyone around the stage were impressive. But it bothered me because I became very aware of these elements. After awhile I kept thinking I was looking at a series of Hallmark greeting cards come to life.

A: You mean it was precious and obvious!

Q: Yes. How do you avoid that?

A: It sounds as if the director was in freeze-frame too long. What I mean by that is that he held the picturization in tableau for long periods of time.

Q: That's true. After a stage picture evolved it stayed there until I was sick of looking at it.

A: It's easy for the director to fall in love with his own picture-making skills, but if you are staging the action of a scene, as we have discussed, you find that the "beats" keep changing, hence the pictures will keep changing. Otherwise, it's like a camera angle that is stationary, and no intercutting takes place to energize the scene.

Q: Well, the musical looked very pretty.

A: Yes, but settling for pretty isn't good enough. I was recently reading an art book on the subject of composition, and the author said its chief virtue is in a sense of repose it gives the viewer. Repose, idleness, peacefulness are anathema to drama, where you want tension, friction, and conflict. Repose can work onstage as contrast, as variation, as a dynamic different than what preceded it and what may come. But pictorial repose for the sake of itself is deadly. Even in a musical.

Q: Can't composition just happen by itself without directorial intervention, so to speak?

A: Absolutely. The subject can dictate it. Actually it should seem so anyway. Things pictorial will sometimes fall into place very nicely if you are on the right road in terms of content. Pictures will happen, the stage will be interestingly composed without your manipulations. It's wonderful when that happens. Everyone is playing strong intentions, listening to each other, the scene has taken off, and you are gripped by the content. You suddenly look at the stage with your visual sense finely attuned and feel wonderment. "Gee, it really looks great!" Yes, that can and does happen. It's like watching spontaneous combustion.

But you can also work to make it happen. When you do, it should always look like it happened by itself.

Q: Can you tell me more about the issue of "reality"?

A: Every play has to be anchored in some kind of reality or other. By *anchored* I mean that it stays located for the audience members. They know where it's at, where it's coming from, so to speak. In a musical like *Carousel*, we go from the real world to heaven when Billy Bigelow dies, then back to the real world. Of course, in *Carousel* the real world, hard as it is for some of the characters, is still presented as a pretty magical place. People sing and dance in ballets and have real, live clam bakes, and we see a beautiful carousel, and everyone is very handsome, lovely, and brimming with Americana. So going to heaven is perfectly consistent in terms of the "reality" that the musical has established. The play from which it is derived, *Liliom*, by Ferenc Molnar, is a very lean, bleak vision of painful love among working-class people. It's the difference between a film noir and an MGM musical.

When an author gives a director her play to do, she holds her breath. She has worked her vision into a particular piece of reality, which is now on the page. She has seen it and heard it and written it down. How will the director and designers realize it on the stage? What reality will they put her play into? Will it be what she saw, or they saw, and how different will it be?

The director, as psychic as he may be, cannot fully get into the author's head, nor should he. He layers his vision of the play on top of the author's. Hopefully the reality that he selects is going to be what the author had in mind. If not, hopefully, the author will say, "Your way of doing it was different than mine, but I like it just as much."

Reality gets into the question of style, which is not the province of this book. Right now reality is mainly a guidepost for the director to know:

What is the world of this play?

How far can I take it?

How far is too far? In other words, when do I start bending reality to the point that I'm doing another play?

Q: It seems that so much depends on staging the action, right?
A: Yes. Keep to that. Doing the simplest thing is always the hardest, that is, reexamining everything in terms of the "basic situation."

STAGING (CONTINUED)

COUNTERPOINT

The staging discussion in the previous chapter focused us on telling one story at a time. *Counterpoint* enables the director to tell more than one story at a time. In music *counterpoint* is defined as "the technique of combining two or more melodic lines in such a way that they establish a harmonic relationship while retaining their linear individuality." In art it is "contrasting but parallel elements."

Counterpoint in the theatre and film is either written into the script and/or provided by the director. Counterpoint has the following values:

1. To contrast different sides of the same narrative.   A painting might have a very jolly picnic scene in the foreground, but in the distance storm clouds are gathering. Because there are literally two moods created at the same time as a result of the difference in atmosphere in each segment of the painting, the viewer is witness to a very active and dramatic story. The storm foreshadows a great change about to take place and gives us a sense of irony that the merry picnickers are unaware that they will soon be drenched in rain. Or the counterpoint can be interpreted another way. The picnic is a celebration because the dark storm clouds have finally moved away.

You might see a scene in a movie where a child is watching a cheerful episode of *Mr. Rogers' Neighborhood* on television in one room and at the same time her parents are being slaughtered by an ax murderer in the next room. The contrast heightens the event and makes it more horrifying.

Shakespeare uses counterpoint by contrasting imagery. In *Romeo and Juliet* a dark night suddenly bursts with "light" after Juliet appears on her balcony. Later in the play while it is still day, Juliet invokes night to hurry up and get there so that she can possess her lover in the dark.

> Come, gentle night; come, loving, black-browed night;
> Give me my Romeo; and, when he shall die,
> Take him and cut him out in little stars,
> And he will make the face of heaven so fine
> That all the world will be in love with night
> And pay no worship to the garish sun . . .

In Chekhov's famous opening of *The Sea Gull*, Masha is asked why she always wears black, and she replies, "I am in mourning for my life." Counterpoint cuts through this scene in two ways:

- Medvedenko is in love with Masha, but Masha is in love with Trepleff. Medvedenko is expressing his need for Masha, but she is longing after Trepleff, who is completely unconcerned about her because he's crazy about Nina.
- Masha is ruthlessly cold and frank about how emotionally removed she is from the man wooing her. Later Nina will behave in exactly the same way toward Trepleff.

Counterpoint permeates the entire play. Themes run in and out, crisscross and finally come together. Two ideas, two aspects of one story are brought together in the title alone. *The Sea Gull* is the part of us that we allow to be free. It's our creative side. It is also the part of us that we are capable of destroying. There are at least two levels of tonality counterpointing each other in the play at the same time: a comedy of unrequited love, preposterous artistic ambitions, selfishness, and childish behavior colliding with the seriousness of failed ambitions, gunshots, dead sea gulls, and suicide.

2. To tell separate narratives either concurrently or alternately.

The British playwright Alan Ayckbourn will often take a number of plots that are taking place in various households and put them all together on one set. None of the different families is aware of each other, even when they are in the same room. Each story overlaps as contrast or augmentation of an overall idea. It's like listening to an orchestra when each section is playing something else.

Counterpoint abounds in many films. Take William Wyler's *The Best Years of Our Lives,* which is easily rentable and should be observed for its examples of counterpoint on many levels:

- Interlocking different stories: The lives of three servicemen returning from World War II weave in and out of each other as the men try to adjust to civilian life. The woman in each man's life is strongly contrasted in terms of her expectations and frustrations. The stories contrast to each other. Each story strengthens the others, so much so that no one story can stand alone.

- Contrasting situations: In the opening section Dana Andrews is an air force captain who has just returned from the war and is trying to get onto a plane. A civilian carrying golf clubs, who is obviously going on a vacation and who hasn't been in the war, gets onto the plane instead. This counterpoint demonstrates the difference between those who served and those who stayed home to play, but more importantly, it foreshadows the difficulty of trying to reenter civilian life.

- Juxtaposing comedy: Fredric March and Myrna Loy are awkward and pained to be with each other after a long separation. They go out on the town to have some fun. There is a long drunken episode that breaks the tension that everyone feels. The comedy is counterpoint to what is really going on underneath the many relationships that are happening by now. Counterpoint helps the characters play against their subtext. What they are really undergoing emotionally or psychologically is covered; they don't play into it or allow others to see what's really going on. This technique heightens the dramatic tension for the audience and makes the comedy a relief on the one hand, while it intensifies the drama on the other.

- Visual intensification: In an office that looks out onto what used to be a little drug store that has expanded to a department store, Dana Andrews is trying to get his old job back. He is a decorated war hero, needing work, but it is clear that he hasn't the temperament to work in this kind of business setting. How do we know? Everything he says contrasts to the setting of the store that the director is showing us: a mecca of commerce and quick sales. The atmosphere is counterpointed by the character's personality, and we fear the worst, which is that he will get the job and fail miserably. Both happen.

At one point there is a cheerful scene with Hogey Carmichael and Harold Ross playing "Chopsticks" on the piano as Fredric March looks on. In the background we see Dana Andrews on the telephone. He is breaking off his relationship with a woman he cares a great deal about, Fredric March's daughter. As a phone scene alone it would be effective. Or a light scene at the piano with the three men would be charming. But cementing the action together in one shot, the three men in the foreground and Dana Andrews way in the background, is a very powerful use of counterpoint.

The Problem of Focus

Counterpoint is a visual and aural narrative that supplements what the audience is seeing and hearing, and as such its use is a matter of focus. "What do I want the audience members to be watching and listening to? When do I want them to shift their eyes to another part of the stage? For how long? At what point do I bring their eyes to something else?" Counterpoint is very subtle. One can watch the scene with the three men at the piano in *The Best Years of Our Lives* and miss Dana Andrews in the background on the telephone. But the shot is composed in such a way that the audience knows that something else is going on underneath the scene whether it sees it or not.

Onstage, where the frame is much larger than a screen or a painting and harder to control because there aren't close-ups or portraits, focus has to be continually shifted in a very organized way. It's easy to alter light cues, easier still to throw in contrasting sound effects, but when you begin staging one group of actors in a certain action, while another group is activated in a different way, things get complicated. Challenging, interesting, but complicated. Tyrone Guthrie was the master of counterpoint. He could have an intimate love scene in the center of the stage, while the entire English army was upstage preparing for war. Each section was designed to heighten the other. The scene that he wanted you to watch was helped enormously by the counterpoint of another scene running at the same time. You always knew where to look, and you had a sense of at least two stories being clearly told.

Exercises

1. Four actors, two couples. Set up two adjoining hotel rooms. Each room has a different story. Even though the time frame is the same, one room can have the TV announcing a national catastrophe, and in the other room jazz is playing on the radio. In room A a couple are getting dressed to go out. In room B a couple are getting undressed to go to bed. Let the actors improvise the situation. As they do, carefully observe them. Whom are you watching? Is one scene blurring the other? Did you miss an important piece of action because you were looking at the wrong place? Do the scene again. Now, because you can't improvise the same thing twice (it's no longer an improv at that point), ask the actors in each room to do the reverse activity. Look at it again. Now you'll begin to see that if you can delay a move in the room on the left, you'll be able to concentrate on what is going on in the room on the right. You may see that if someone on the left moves in a certain direction, it will throw focus onto the person you want to see in the room on the right. After a story develops, write it down, give it back to the actors, and organize the staging in order to control the focus between the rooms. When you have finished staging the scene, run it through to see if your eyes are traveling to the right place at the right time. If not, redo the blocking until you are satisfied. At this point you might want both rooms to receive the news of the external catastrophe at the same time and see how this affects each scene.

2. Ask the actors to come up with something that you do not suspect. Each scene will have a surprise element. You don't know what it is, and the actors in the other scene don't know what it is. See what happens when the surprise element happens because it will be something that you really want to see. When you were watching it, did the activity in the other room add to it or detract from it? Now, go back and direct the staging always with the intention of keeping the eyes of the audience where you want them focused.

- Keep dialogue to a minimum. Because the rooms are separated, the actors will need very specific verbal cues from the room opposite to execute their blocking and business.
- All the moves have to be synchronized with precise timing. The moves in counterpoint have to bring focus onto what the main action is at the moment. When the main action shifts to

the other room, focus has to be brought there by the room that was just in focus. It's as though there were a ball, and each actor or couple was carrying it until time to pass it to the other couple. As a matter of fact, you can do this as an exercise. Have the actors in one room toss the ball to the actors in the next as focus passes back and forth. You might see that the actors will manage to get themselves into the right position with just the right timing to pass the ball.

TONE, MOOD, AND ATMOSPHERE

The pictures that the audience sees, the compositions that subliminally affect it, the use of counterpoint all can be meaningful on a conscious level or quite suggestive. Not to get too fancy, there is a kind of evocative poetry that these elements can create such as tone, mood, and atmosphere. Worlds within worlds are capable of happening on-stage: A composition suggests an atmosphere, certain pictures reflect a mood, changing tonalities can come from the use of counterpoint. But sometimes the director has other tools to get to these aspects of production.

Tone

I don't know which is worse: staging a rip-roaring farce and not getting any laughs or staging a tragedy and getting laughs in the wrong places. I've experienced both.

Tone lets the audience know what it's watching—a comedy, a tragedy, a melodrama, a romance, and so forth. In the musical *A Funny Thing Happened on the Way to the Forum* the tone or mood is set by the song, "Comedy Tonight," which, combined with the way it can be staged, lets you know that you are going to watch lots of girls, old-fashioned burlesque, improbable antics, and comic routines, so start laughing. It gives signals and guideposts immediately so that the audience knows how to take the show.

The song "Comedy Tonight" wasn't always in that show and came in after the audience wasn't laughing. But it's a classic example of setting the tone of a show as soon as you can. And I'd say that whenever you're directing a comedy there's got to be some equivalent of "Comedy Tonight" up front.

The question often emerges about shifts of tone. In other words, can a show go from a serious tone to a comedic one, then back again? Yes. Many current plays do that. Come to think of it, Chekhov does that in the sense of demonstrating the absurdity of various characters dealing with serious issues.

Shakespeare often shifts tonality. There can be a scene at court with great pomp and gravity followed by a band of merry fools in a tavern. The director stages each scene as it fully deserves, shifting the dynamics of tone like a home movie that one minute shows you someone who has slipped on a banana peel and the next minute shows you the person in traction in the hospital.

How you modulate your staging depends on what sense of reality you want. I've seen the major Chekhov plays directed as tragedies, directed as comedies, directed as swinging back and forth between each. This isn't to say that the serious versions had more reality. For me, they had less. I think comedy is always more serious than so-called serious theatre. It's harder to do, but it's truer. That's my personal outlook, obviously. If I want reality, I bring out what's funny and ridiculous. I hope at the same time that I'm bringing out what's moving and human.

Exercise: Stage the Opening Chorus of Stephen Sondheim's *Sweeney Todd:*

> Attend the tale of Sweeney Todd.
> His skin was pale and his eye was odd.
> He shaved the faces of gentlemen
> Who never thereafter were heard of again.
> He trod a path that few have trod,
> Did Sweeney Todd.
> The Demon Barber of Fleet Street.

The tone of the lyrics and the music that accompanies them is macabre. A story about a strange man and his victims is declaimed. The original stage directions are about grave diggers digging, getting lost inside the graves, and reemerging as the chorus enters. The director can go along with this and establish a tone that is immediately chilling and forbidding or, quite to the contrary, can stage a very playful atmosphere with children skipping and playing games. This tone is lighter, less sententious, less macabre than grave diggers, and it might be more effective because it gives the show further to go: We travel from children singing to bloody retribution and darkness.

Or try it any way you please and see where your audience feels it's being led.

Atmosphere

We know from watching countless TV police shows how atmosphere in the police station is created. Lots of movement in the background by very busy people, overlapping dialogue, phones ringing constantly, sirens heard in the distance, cell doors clanging, hoodlums in handcuffs brought in, detectives at their desks eating out of paper bags and drinking from cardboard containers through straws. Rearrange a few of the details, put the actors into different clothes, and we are watching a hospital show.

All of these details are comforting to the audience, which needs this kind of familiarity week after week. The atmosphere locates the event and adds to it. It has the "ring of truth" for its audience.

Onstage atmosphere can be suggested in a single stroke. The details of reality demanded in film or TV are not necessary because that kind of realism is neither expected nor affordable; and without close-ups all that clutter makes focus impossible. In the theatre a single bench, a beam of light that suggests the moon, and the sound of recorded crickets suggest an evening in the country.

Atmosphere gives a distinct sense of time, place, weather. In a way, it has to do with scenery and has nothing to do with scenery, depending on your aesthetic. If you are a director who prefers minimalism and artistic economy, you can convey atmosphere on a bare stage with actors alone, just through your staging. Weather can be imagined and played as something real. The actors can be slipping around on imaginary ice. They can be climbing imaginary mountains. They can be dying of thirst in an imaginary desert.

Or, depending on your point of view and budget, you can have real sand all over the stage and do the same thing.

The benefit of atmosphere is that it heightens the objectives and obstacles of the characters. The heat in *Cat on a Hot Tin Roof* sears through Maggie and ignites her desires and thwarts her at the same time. For some reason atmosphere is often ignored in student productions where you see characters talking about the cold but behaving like they're in a warm theatre; talking about the rainstorm that they just came through but playing as though not a drop hit them outside; talking about what a strange place the room is, yet seeming to know exactly where everything is located.

If your staging doesn't dramatize the inherent atmosphere of the script, you are working against the reality of the circumstances and asking your audience members to do too much work, which means that they will be trying to fill in what you've left out. Audiences are very nice this way. They'll go a long way, pretending that you've given them things that you haven't.

Mood

Lighting, music, sound effects, setting, character behavior, and staging help convey a mood.

The mood of most sitcoms is bright and cheerful. The sets are as colorful as the characters. The aim is to put the audience in a happy, laughing frame of mind.

There is the so-called Chekhovian mood, which is supposed to be very wistful, sad, and Russian. To many people this means that the characters are unhappy about the way their lives have turned out and cry a lot. This mood is created by dark lighting, atmospheric sounds of the country, peasants singing in the background, and a lot of sitting around in very pastoral outdoor settings or in freezing rooms.

Certain directors seem to bring mood with them wherever they go. Tyrone Guthrie's work on classic plays put me in a mood of great joy and exhilaration. Michael Langham, who succeeded Guthrie at Stratford, Ontario, brought out mellow textures of the same plays. I used to think of his work as "autumnal." In Bob Fosse's choreography the mood was Broadway and jazz and very, very cynical and tough.

Mood can be enhanced by underscored music. You'll notice when you are doing a play licensed by Samuel French or Dramatists Play Service that there is often a recording of the original music that you can rent. The music was either played under scenes or used as filler during scene changes in the original production. I know a director who went so overboard on underscoring that he hired a composer who put music underneath every line of dialogue. This was the opposite of the audience members doing all the work. Here, they had no work to do at all. Whatever was left for them to figure out was told to them by the music. Also, music (and this is my own bias), unless used very judiciously, can be very manipulative. Music, even wall-to-wall music, works in the movies, because half the time we aren't aware of its pull on us. But in the theatre the audience is always conscious of it.

Exercises

1. Present a ten-minute piece that reeks of mood and atmosphere. A storyline in the narrative or logical sense is not necessary. You can use material from a play or a dream. Use whatever technical effects you can get your hands on. The main idea is to explore mood and atmosphere as tools to enhance staging.

2. Take a scene commonly associated with these elements and remove them. Do an anti-Chekhovian Chekhov scene. No sadness, no tears, no melancholy. Explore any other approach.

   Do the ghost scene from *Hamlet* without the following traditional effects: night, fog, sound of the sea, green or grey makeup on Hamlet's father, his voice magnified, strange lighting, and so forth. Use this assignment to employ mood and atmosphere in your own way, unlike anything anyone has ever seen before.

Note: Of course, this is what you always want to do. You know what the traditional ways have been, but your work is to create something completely original. I've always had queasy feelings about directors who say, "I'll steal anything that's any good." There are directors who have been very successful taking parts of other people's work. They'll take an entire concept from Strehler in Italy, a staging from Peter Brook, a style from Mnouchkine, anything from Brecht (who stole from everyone himself), a little from Grotowski, and a few things from the butcher, the baker, the candlestick maker. Often these directors are far more successful than the people they've stolen from.

STAGING ON OPEN STAGES

FREQUENTLY ASKED QUESTIONS

Q: What is an open stage?

A: An open stage has no proscenium—that archway between the audience and the stage that held the action inside a picture frame is gone. The audience usually is seated wrapped around a stage that is in the shape of a semicircle such as the Greek theatre or that thrusts farther into the audience like the Elizabethan theatre. This configuration is sometimes referred to as "three-quarter thrust." There is also full arena, which can be a square or a circle or an oblong and is similar to a sports arena. The audience in both three-quarter and full arena is usually banked in tiers, high above the players in order to get the fullest view of every part of the action. The following examples are by the designer Karl Eigsti. One is from our production of John Arden's *Sgt. Musgrave's Dance* at the Tyrone Guthrie Theatre; the other is from Eugene O'Neill's *Long Day's Journey into Night* at Arena Stage.

Sgt. Musgrave's Dance takes place at a colliery in a mining town in the north of England. Although we removed the Elizabethan inner above and inner below that were part of the original concept of the stage, we replaced them with a variation. (See drawing of stage on page 178.) Note the scaling of the design. Because the Guthrie stage is such a huge cube of space it's easy to lose the characters onstage. The use of the inner above narrows our field of vision, and the action becomes more intimate.

The man downstage, holding the lantern, has his back to the center of the audience, but his face is seen perfectly by the remaining sides of the house. The groundplan rakes the objects onstage along diagonal lines, helping the majority of the house to see most of the action. Compositionally, there is a triangle downstage made by the three figures. The apex of the triangle is the man with the lantern, who is throwing focus up to the man on the above. The guard with the rifle upstage-right is balanced by the mass down-left. The straps of the huge wheel tend, in this rendering, to move the eyes of the audience off-left, but that did not happen because of the way they were lit.

Karl Eigðtið ðrawing of Sgt. Musgrave's Dance *ðtage.*

A few things to notice in the *Long Day's Journey into Night* illustration (see drawing on page 179): The play is a modern tragedy, and what we wanted most of all was to create a very stark, minimalistic world where human action and language could be played. Although

Karl Eigstis drawing of Long Day's Journey into Night *stage.*

the groundplan represents rooms in a house, there are no walls or partitions to indicate separation. The scaling of the set is affected by the shutters that you see hanging below the light grid. Our field of vision is narrowed by them, and our focus stays with the actors on the stage, but there is an epic size to the experience.

The playing areas are set up on a diagonal axis. The two people at the dining room table are playing over each other's shoulder to open each player to at least two tiers.

You can see Mary Tyrone entering via the vomitorium on the lower left side of the drawing. Some of the audience members will see her there, some won't. It depends on how you light her. These are the final moments of the play, and you need to decide at what point you want the entire house to see her. As you can see, two characters onstage are about to notice her. After one of them or both of them see her, they will shift the focus of the audience onto her entrance. The final impact of her entrance will come from the man whose back is to us. The audience will be waiting to see his reaction to her.

Q: What's the advantage of this arrangement of the stage and the audience?

A: Having worked at both Arena Stage in Washington, D.C., for many years and at the Guthrie Theatre in its early days, I'd say the advantages are the following:

1. The picture framing of the proscenium is viewed from only one side—where everyone is seated. The arena allows events to play on stage in a much freer form. I used to like to quote Zelda Fichandler, the founder of Arena Stage, who would say, "Life is in the round." I believe what she meant by that is that experience is open to more than one perspective. Experience also happens all around us. Staging in the arena, to quote Mrs. Fichandler again, "provides infinite variability in terms of plasticity and movement."

2. The Guthrie Theatre was modeled and refined on its predecessor in Stratford, Ontario. The stage thrusts into the house and is platformed around a moat.

Writing about building the theatre in Minneapolis, Guthrie says:

> . . . more people can be got into the same amount of cubic space if they are seated around an open stage, rather than facing a proscenium. When folded around an open stage none of them need sit farther away than the fourteenth row, approximately fifty feet from the middle of the stage. If you are going to offer the sort of program that demands the serious concentration of the audience, then it is essential that actor and audience be brought into the closest possible mutual contract.
>
> But to my mind even more important is the fact that the proscenium stage is deliberately designed to encourage the audience to believe that events on stage are "really" taking place, to accept a palpable fiction for fact; whereas the open

stage discourages "illusion" and emphasizes that a play is a ritual in which the audience is invited to participate.

Finally, apart from these technical or philosophical considerations, we believed it would be a good idea to have an open stage simply because it was not the obvious, conventional kind. It would stress, we felt, the experimental and pioneering character of the whole venture; it would be more of a talking point; and, by providing a more three-dimensional entertainment, would emphasize the contrast between the live theatre and movies or TV. This contrast is less marked when a play is framed by a rectangular proscenium, like the rectangular movie or TV screen.

Q: Wasn't Guthrie's interest primarily the classical theatre?

A: Yes, I believe that the philosophy that Guthrie and his designer, Tanya Moiseiwitsch had concerning their stage had a great deal to do with their feelings about classical theatre. They worked in a highly lyrical and romantic style. There were lots of armies, drums, banners, trumpets, cannons belching smoke, and great language that filled the theatre with poetry. You always felt that these spectacles were tumbling from the stage onto your lap. More important, you felt something heroic and meaningful about the grandeur of the human spirit.

Q: And scenery? How does that differ on open stages?

A: Originally, both Stratford and the Guthrie were Elizabethan models with an inner above and inner below. The great wooden floor of the stage was its most important scenic element because everyone was sitting above it, and that's what people saw. If there was any scenery, it was emblematic. A chandelier of a certain period, a table, a chair told you what world you were in. The productions were dominated by costumes. These costumes set against the dark floor were the palette that the play worked on. There was no need for literal scenery. Hence, there was no need for stage mechanics and massive set changes from scene to scene. The audience could imagine where it was with one or two suggestions.

Arena Stage started from the same spirit, but scenery became very elaborate after it moved into its large theatre, where the stage is completely mechanized and used to spectacular effect.

Later, the use of scenery at the Guthrie changed as well because although only a wooden floor, an inner above, an inner below, and a few pieces were fine for classical plays, they did not work for contemporary plays. And as the repertoire expanded the concepts of scenery, reality, and artistic needs changed with it. *Illusion*, a word that Guthrie said he hated, was warmly greeted by him after he saw the versatility of the stage that he helped create.

Q: Are some plays better than others on the open stage?

A: That's a matter of great debate. Some directors believe that certain kinds of comedies cannot be played on an open stage because the jokes and humor need a frontal assault, so to speak. Other directors can't see how you can do a musical in the arena form:

Where do you put the orchestra?

How does the conductor cue the singers?

How many sides can you sing to at one time, given the fact that you have only one head?

Q: My own opinion is that there is no limit to the repertoire that can be successfully put onto an open stage. And as for musicals, many cities have summer musical tents in the arena form.

Q: Are there some *dos* and *don'ts* about the open stage?

A: First avoid the traps:

1. Actors bellowing the lines. Often you will see a lot of spewing of saliva from the actor's mouth as he overaspirates in an attempt to be heard. Listening to the performance gets to be like listening to instruments that can play only loud. Sound is never modulated for variation and color. The actors seem to feel that because people are sitting behind them, they have to shout, hoping that their voices carry over their shoulders. In the early days of the Guthrie, actors used to talk about "diaphragmatic pressure": how much air they needed to take in to get the sound out. It's not necessary to produce this much sound unless the acoustics of the house are faulty.

2. "Making the rounds." This is when the actor ceaselessly roams the stage from one side to the other in order for all sides to take him in. This, of course, never happened in a Tyrone Guthrie show, but it was the house style of the Shake-

speare Festival in Central Park and of many other theatres at one time. (It was also ironic that the festival miked its actors anyway, so all this staging that had the actor going from side to the other was unnecessary to begin with.)

"Making the rounds" was a solution to a problem that created a worse problem. Let's say that you are sitting in a tier facing the actor. The actor is speaking in your direction. You hear her. But then she leaves your direction and moves to the next tier. You hear her a little less. She moves farther away, facing another tier of seats, and you've lost her completely. Then she comes back in your direction. It's like a shortwave radio signal that is coming in and out with a lot of interference.

3. Playing to the critics. The director knows where members of the press will be seated opening night and aims the show in their direction. The critics do not sit just anywhere. They want the "best seats," and management wants to put them there. This knowledge tempts the director to stage the show like it's on a proscenium. You will often see productions where the audience on either side of the stage or to the extreme sides is fully cheated. I, myself, have been seated behind chairs, behind vases on tables and behind actors a good deal of the evening. Backstage I didn't recognize one of the actresses because I hadn't seen her face all evening. The press had its center seats for one night, while someone sat in my seat every night for thirty performances.

The director and the actors need to be aware of:

1. The stage in every scene has to be "shared." Usually the actors play across each other's shoulders diagonally, in very much the same way that a two-shot in a film is photographed. If you are in full arena, almost each tier gets a good view of either actor. This is very different than proscenium staging, where, if an actor moves onto another plane above you, you are upstaged. There is no way you can be upstaged in arena, unless you end up playing with your head facing one of the vomitoriums, which are the tunnels that give access to and from the stage.

   In general, playing on the diagonal is one of the secrets of the open stage.

2. In the proscenium, center stage is a favored position. It's regarded as very strong in terms of the sight lines of the house and is a natural point of visual focus for the audience. You'll notice that concerts, recitals, major songs in musicals often are played there. On a three-quarter stage, you have to find alternatives to playing major events center stage. *Center* often means cutting off a large segment of the house at either side.

3. The tendency to go farther upstage so that more of the house can see the actor has the effect of distancing the audience from the actor.

Q: Should the director move around a lot, checking how the show is looking from each side?

A: Yes. If you don't have in your head the spatial sense of how it's looking from each tier, which is very difficult at first, you owe it to your audience and your actors to get out of your chair and see what the show looks like from all points of view. Especially when you're doing run-throughs, sit in one section and see how the show is playing from that perspective.

Q: People say the problem with the open stage is that, depending on where your seat is, you are going to see a different show than the person on the other side of the stage will see. Is this true?

A: Let me answer this way. I find watching plays on the open stage very exciting because it's inherently a more dynamic and energetic form.

Q: What do you mean by that?

A: The open stage gives the audience a sense of watching a play in three dimensions. It is very much like watching a sports event where the ball is continually in play, and the players can go all over the court or the rink as they play the game. The open stage, especially arena, frees the action from the demand of playing to one side. I think there's just one rule about the open stage, which is to share the play with as much of the house as possible and not to exclude any section, at least not for any period of time. This doesn't mean "doing the rounds." Instead, it means finding creative ways of moving and shaping the stage action almost like a choreographer. You have to think as if you're sculpting in space with the actors.

However, you can get a different show with staging that's still rooted in a proscenium mode. Talking about three-quarter staging that she has seen, Zelda Fichandler has said, "I have noticed that plays in this form have been designed, sculpted, directed, and acted more or less from the 'front,' the aesthetic weight of the rear wall finally prevailing. When I have sat on the 'sides' I have not merely seen the play differently, I have seen the sides of the play. That is, the experience of the play—intellectually and sensually—has been weakened. I think this is a correct observation and surely it is borne out by the pricing policy of these theatres: The most expensive seats splay out from the tongue of the stage; the cheaper seats edge around the stage toward the architectural wall at the back of it."

Q: You mean that more movement is usually the norm on an open stage?

A: I think so. Of course, the movement has to be justified, it has to be in the style or reality that you've selected to work in. But first get the scene right. Find what's going on within it and what the best way is to stage the action. After that, you will find certain adjustments that will open it up to more of the audience. You don't have to go into rehearsal hysterically thinking: "My god, I've got four sides to play to and only two actors in this scene, which is fairly static to begin with!" But after you've gotten the scene to work, it's important that you let the whole house share it. I've sat in the north tier at Arena Stage and have had a wonderful show presented to me, knowing that no one in the south tier was able to see what I was seeing because the director had left that tier out. I've also seen shows in three-quarter that were staged just like proscenium plays and left out several hundred people who were watching the show on the sides.

The glory of working the open stage is that you can open up a scene in ways that you couldn't possibly do on a proscenium, with moves, with pieces of business, with reactions that don't have to play in one direction. After I've done something on an open stage it would seem like putting it into a box if it had to transfer to proscenium. (As a matter of fact, I've experienced this.)

Q: But back to my question. Every tier is getting a different show, isn't it? In your example of the south tier at Arena, the show that those viewers got was the backs of the actors and not much of the dialogue, most likely.

A: Even in the best stagings, the show is, I have to admit, slightly different, yes. The question is "different worse" or "different better"? I've sat on the extreme sides of some of my own productions and liked them much better. Was it a different play than what another section was getting? I don't know. On the proscenium we are getting the master shot. On the open stage we can get close-ups, different angles, long shots, depending on where we are sitting and how the staging is laid out before us.

For example, two characters in a comedy scene. One of the characters has a line that is a joke. A big laugh is expected. Let's say that you've staged it so that upon telling the joke, the actor "walks out of the laugh." This is when an actor says a joke and moves away. This heightens the laugh because it's so outrageously funny for the audience to watch the actor deliver this unexpected, outrageous line and to see him walk away like nothing has happened. On a proscenium this would get a laugh. In arena, it can also get the same laugh because there is a whole tier of people watching him come their way after he has delivered the joke, behaving as though he has said nothing out of the ordinary. There is another tier watching the "take" or the reaction of the other actor who has received this joke. And if you've staged it diagonally, each actor will be getting a good shot of at least two tiers fully seeing him.

Q: Doesn't the lighting appear to be different from each side?

A: Yes, that's a disappointment. From the center it might seem like night, and from another angle, if you're sitting near the hot spots, it can look like day.

Q: What about counterpoint? Isn't it easier to control on a proscenium?

A: Because Guthrie was practically its inventor, you can be sure that counterpoint works very successfully in three-quarter. The background or the far wall is a backdrop that becomes a canvas for the director to paint against. There is also the use of the stairs around the stage and the moat for all kinds of incidental and parallel action. In the arena form, counterpoint is possible but more of a challenge. It can be like a three-ring

An example of a thrust stage where part of the audience is "excluded" from the action.

An example of an arena stage and its "excluded" audience.

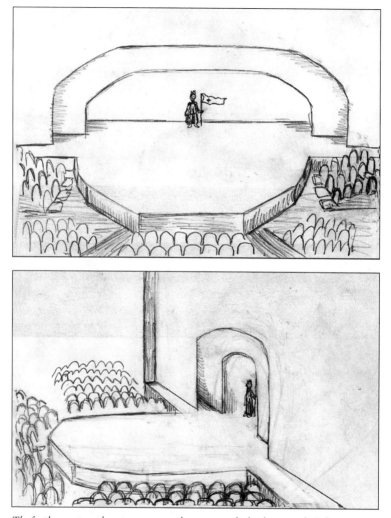

The further upstage the actor goes on a thrust stage, the farther away he is from a great deal of the audience.

circus that has to be focused. Aside from staging, focus can be helped by:

1. Lighting and use of levels.   One of the principles of the open stage before these theatres became so scenery happy was the minimal use of sets with a maximum of artistic economy. Lighting, in that case, served many functions, especially picking out areas where scenes were being played. The action could jump from place to place by lighting. There was no need to bring on tons of scenery to tell the story. Actors could be on a bare stage doing a scene, there could be a blackout, and the lights would come up on another part of the stage, implying another scene, another place, and another time.

Depending on sight lines, levels can be used, which denote different playing spaces for different geographic locations in the story. These levels also help with focusing action if you have a multiplicity of events taking place at the same time.

2. Action around the perimeter of where central action is occurring. I like to think of this as a kind of visual *obbligato* or accompaniment. And just as in music, this accompanies the main action as either complementary or contrasting, as discussed in the section on counterpoint. You'll often hear an actor say, "Is she going to do that while I'm doing my speech?" This means that the actor has just noticed that another character is moving or doing a piece of business while he's doing his speech. In the old school of acting, no one was supposed to breathe, let alone move, while the star or leading players were "acting." They didn't want to be upstaged by upstarts, which means someone else getting the focus. There are many famous stories of how actors have tripped up and foiled one another onstage. However, the director wants to keep the stage alive. She can't have a stage full of actors frozen every time the lead opens his mouth. If you are trying to counterpoint an important speech by using another action to throw down focus to it, the actor doing that speech has to know that the movement and action are there to help him, not to thwart him. But actors will be actors, and you have to make sure that that little scene used to counterpoint the main one doesn't assume epic proportions by the third performance, especially on an open stage, where it will be close to an audience of its own.

3. Sound is a very powerful instrument in arena, especially if the setting is minimal or not literal.   Sound will anchor the audience in a reality. You don't need to see rain, just hear it, to feel what the weather is like. Also, sound can travel around an arena house more effectively than it can in a proscenium house because geography isn't always that literal, either. In the proscenium a door can represent the outside of a house. In the arena there are rarely doors because they impede sight lines. Outside the house can be all around the audience. If a lion has escaped from the zoo, he is prowling around in the round, not just prowling very specifically behind a door. Again, because it's less literal, the open stage offers a wider range for the director as well as for the audience to experience events very imaginatively.

Q: How do I get to experience working on the open stage?
A: Reconfigure your classroom or workshop so that the audience is not seated conventionally. Start with a few scenes. Make sure that when the scenes are presented you have people sitting in each section. As part of the critique ask what each section missed, if anything.
    Try a one-act play in either three-quarter thrust or arena. Work out the groundplan, that is, where you are going to place the set pieces. Check to see that the sight lines are clear from all sides as much as possible. Stage the play.
Q: Do I have to run around the room, from side to side, as I'm blocking to make sure that everything is being seen properly?
A: Not until you've run through. Stay in one place, concentrate on the play and your work with the actors, but be aware of where your audience is going to be seated.
Q: Maybe I shouldn't be aware of the audience at all, just try to forget about it. What do you think?
A: I know directors who forget the audience, and it's not a good idea. They become the audience and see the show only from where they're sitting in rehearsal. I don't think a director has to concern himself with what the audience is going to think or feel or how it will react to the show. To that extent you don't have to think of the audience at all. But you have to be aware of where audience members are sitting and of how much of what's going onstage they can see.

CHECKLIST

Focus

Q: Where do you want the audience to look?
How long do you want the focus to be in one place?
When do you want the focus to change to another character or another place?

Counterpoint

Q: In your working counterpoint have you:
Overemphasized the secondary scene, or is the primary scene still in focus?
Maneuvered the stage action so that the audience is visually following the shifts from one scene to the other?
Made sure that the contrasts between scenes and characters are dynamic enough, or does everything seem to be blending into the same textures?
Been able to look at films, observing the technique?

Tone

Q: Have you worked the first fifteen minutes of the show so that the tone you want to set is there? In other words, will the audience know what kind of show it's watching?
Are you at the place in rehearsal where it's a comedy but nothing is funny anymore? Will inventing fresh business help?

Mood

Q: Is your staging reflecting any mood at all, or are you waiting for the scenery and lighting designer to do the job?
How important is mood to your piece?
Is your use of music and sound adequate or too much? Do they enhance the work or get in the way of it by being too obvious?

Atmosphere

Q: Are you and the actors playing the physical realities and circumstances?

How necessary is atmosphere for what you're trying to achieve?

Would eliminating it completely make things cleaner and simpler?

Open Stages

Q: Have you avoided bellowing actors and "making the rounds"?

How much is each side being cheated? Can you correct it?

Is there a tendency for the actors to still play on the same plane, or are they working diagonally and across the shoulders in order to open them up?

Have you cured yourself of "prosceniumitis," which means that your staging is partially for the round and partially for the proscenium? Can you break the ties that bind you and free yourself from that picture frame?

CHAPTER ELEVEN

CONCEPTS

In this chapter we are going to look at the diaries (fictional) of two directors. Each director has a very different way of working, and each director has a very different concept. The term *concept* has come to mean many things. It can mean the scheme of production that the director and the designers have evolved. It can mean an idea that has strong intellectual, theoretical, or literary significance and how that idea is to be represented. Basically, I like to think of *concept* simply as "how the director sees it."

The first diary is by a young woman named Meg. She decided to direct Edward Albee's one-act play, *The Zoo Story*. The other diary, which we'll come to later, is by a student named Ted, who attempted to turn Ibsen's *A Doll's House* into a musical of sorts.

THE DIARY OF A DIRECTOR

Dear friend,

Let me introduce myself. I'm a director. Female. Late twenties. I love the theatre and hope the theatre loves me. I don't have that much experience directing and have chosen Albee's *The Zoo Story* as my project this year. Let me get to my concept straightaway.

I want this play to be so real that it will make the audience run out of the theatre in terror! I want nothing artificial or stagy or theatrical about it. I want nothing but real life on stage. As a matter of fact, I wish I didn't have to do it in a theatre. I was thinking of doing the play in the park with the audience on blankets, but there are too many distractions out there.

What I want to see onstage is "nowness." That means immediacy, something that is happening before our eyes. I want the audience to witness a horrifying event. One that will shake it up and not let it off the hook!

I want complete realism, *verismo*, cinema verité.

That's the concept, at least. Now, how do I achieve it? (They don't teach that part here. Rather, they let you figure it out yourself.)

Before going any further I'm going to make a checklist now and see after the show is over if I adhered to any of it. Here goes.

Meg's Big List

1. Stick with your concept to the bitter end.
2. Keep working out the story of the play until I get it straight, clear, and to the point.
3. Locate what the play is about, so that the production will have a strong center and I, as the director, will be grounded.
4. Cast two of the best actors I can find.
5. Be specific in all my choices in working with them.
6. Keep an atmosphere of exploration in rehearsal so that the actors will feel free to try anything, use their imaginations and themselves in as open a way as possible.
7. Which reminds me: use myself, my own experiences, and how I relate to this play. I don't want to get all intellectual and mushy about things.
8. I want a kinetic experience for the audience.

Let me tell you a bit about the plot of the play. Peter, an ordinary fellow, is spending a lazy Sunday afternoon, sitting on a bench in Central Park, reading a book, when a strange fellow, named Jerry, enters asking for directions. But he wants more than directions, he wants to engage Peter in a conversation. It turns out that Jerry needs an audience for what's bothering him. Although we see that he is disturbed and keeps referring to something that just happened at the zoo, we're not exactly sure what his problem is. In a very long speech called "The Story of Jerry and the Dog," he reveals how his landlady's dog had always attempted to attack him whenever he came home to his building. Jerry always managed to escape unscathed. At one point he brought the dog hamburgers, which he laid down in the hallway. The dog would eat the meat, then attack him. Finally he tried murdering the dog by putting rat poison in a hamburger. The dog became very ill but survived, and since then a kind of truce has formed between the man and the animal. They just stare at each other now, and after awhile the dog walks away, indifferent to Jerry. Jerry speculates that the dog and he have lost all contact with each other and wonders if his feeding the dog had been an act of love on his part and if the dog attacking him had been its attempt at love.

Peter has been disturbed by this story and states that he doesn't understand any of it. Enraged, Jerry starts punching him in the arm and demanding the bench for himself. Peter refuses out of righteous indignation. Jerry starts hitting him harder, and Peter is ready to fight it out physically. They rise, and Jerry takes a knife from his pocket, which he tosses at Peter's feet. Provoking Peter to pick up the knife, Jerry impales himself on it in a willful act of suicide. Jerry beseeches Peter to run away in order not to have anything to do with this.

The play is naturalistic. It deals with character behavior. But it also seems to be part of the Absurdist writing of the late fifties and early sixties—Ionesco, Beckett, authors who dramatized man's inability to make connections to others. The only way I can describe it is as "naturalism with a tilt." The basis of the play's anguish comes from a sense of man feeling dislocated from his own environment.

The structure is a cyclical series of arguments: Jerry thrusts, and Peter parries in a continuous duel of wits. Jerry keeps provoking, Peter keeps deflecting, but what starts as fun and games becomes very threatening and out of control with a knife and a dying man.

Mystery helps the dramatic tension: Who is Jerry, what does he really want, is he telling the truth, and is he crazy enough to be dangerous?

Threat of impending tragedy, certainly a threat that Peter is in danger, runs through the play.

There is a unity of time, place, and action. This helps with the inevitability that something momentous is going to take place.

If I want the play to happen in the present tense what I have to examine are:

Turning points.

Recognitions.

Reversals.

Here's the opening dialogue, which illustrates some of the texture of the play and sets its overall pattern:

Central Park, New York City.
As the curtain rises, PETER is seated on the bench stage right. He is reading a book. He stops reading, cleans his glasses, goes back to reading. JERRY enters.

Jerry: I've been to the zoo. (*Peter doesn't notice.*) I said, I've been to the zoo. MISTER, I'VE BEEN TO THE ZOO!

Peter: Hm? . . . What? . . . I'm sorry, were you talking to me?

Jerry: I went to the zoo, and then I walked until I came here. Have I been walking north?

Peter: (*puzzled*) North? Why . . . I . . . I think so. Let me see.

Jerry: (*pointing past the audience*) Is that Fifth Avenue?

Peter: Why yes, yes, it is.

Jerry: And what is that cross street there; that one, to the right?

Peter: That? Oh, that's Seventy-fourth Street.

Jerry: And the zoo is around Sixty-fifth Street; so, I've been walking north.

Peter: (*anxious to get back to his reading*) Yes, it would seem so.

Jerry: GOOD OLD NORTH.

Peter: (*lightly, by reflex*) Ha, ha.

Jerry: But not due north.

Peter: I. . . well, no, not due north; but we . . . call it north. It's northerly.

Jerry: (*watches as PETER, anxious to dismiss him, prepares his pipe*) Well, boy; you're not going to get lung cancer, are you?

Peter: (*looks up, a little annoyed, then smiles*) No, sir. Not from this.

Jerry: No, sir. What you'll probably get is cancer of the mouth, and then you'll have to wear one of those things Freud wore after they took one whole side of his jaw away. What do they call those things?

Peter: (*uncomfortable*) A prosthesis?

Jerry: The very thing! A prosthesis. You're an educated man, aren't you? Are you a doctor?

Peter: Oh, no, no. I read about it somewhere. *Time* magazine, I think.
(*He turns to his book.*)

Jerry: Well, *Time* magazine isn't for blockheads.

Peter: No, I suppose not.

Jerry: Boy, I'm glad that's Fifth Avenue there.

Peter: Yes.

Jerry: I don't like the west side of the park much.

Peter: Oh? (*then, slightly wary, but interested*) Why?

Jerry: (*offhand*) I don't know.

Peter: Oh. (*he returns to his book.*)

Jerry: (*he stands for a few seconds, looking at PETER, who finally looks up again, puzzled.*) Do you mind if we talk?

Peter: (*obviously minding*) Why . . . no, no.

Jerry: Yes, you do; you do.

Peter: (*puts his book down, his pipe out and away, smiling*) No, really; I don't mind.

Jerry: Yes, you do.

Peter: (*finally decided*) No; I don't mind at all, really.

Observation: I wonder if Peter wants the same thing as Jerry: to make contact with another person! Somehow, what the play is about is connected with this idea.

Meg

Dear friend,

We began rehearsals today!

I'm not that crazy about the two actors I've had to cast. They were all that were left from the casting pool. They're nice enough personally, but the fellow playing Jerry thinks he's Al Pacino, whom he adores. The actor playing Peter told me he wished he was playing Jerry. So I now have a Jerry who's playing Al Pacino and a Peter who is playing Jerry.

We read the play, and I wondered if it wasn't too late for me to change my major! It wasn't that bad, but close. Too much acting. The one positive thing I learned, however, is that the play is quite funny, which took me by surprise.

At the end of the reading Al Pacino asked me what my concept was. I told the actors that my concept was to make the play seem so real that there would be no line dividing reality from playmaking. He was particularly delighted and said that's why he loved Pacino's work so much. I said, "Are you aware that your acting is like an imitation of him?" He said that is deliberate. I suggested that he find his own style and that if the audience members became aware that they were watching an imitation of Al Pacino it would alienate them from the play.

I hinted that the actor playing Peter was a little too aggressive in the reading. He said, "I can't sit here like a lump! This character's passive enough, don't I have to fight for something?" I told him that he does, but in Peter's way and at the right time. Otherwise, I have two Jerrys onstage. I suggested that a major reversal in the action was when Peter refused to let Jerry take sole possession of the bench and that he should save that side of Peter's character for that. (He seemed to like that idea.)

We read the play a second time, after I gave this direction. "Let's read the play as simply as possible, with as little acting as possible."

I should have known better. The reading was absolutely dead. They were going through it like zombies, just to convince me of what a wrong direction I had given them. I became very angry but tried not to show it. (I must say that when I'm directing I never know if I should show my anger or repress it completely. Although I think the leadership that remains cool steers the steadiest course.)

I said, "Look, let's not prove a point. It's a waste of time. I'd like to read the play again. This time let's not impose anything on it, okay? Just go with your impulses and try to make something happen between the both of you. Like two guys in a park, not actors. Okay?"

This time the reading was much better. They actually played with each other, and some sparks began to fly. But, of course, whenever either actor was in doubt or lost trust in the process of being simple and true, he would start acting up a storm and revert to a kind of staginess that I just hate, such as long dramatic pauses, effective overuse of certain words, and generalized emoting.

We ended rehearsal discussing the play, and the actor playing Jerry asked a very good question: "How do I find the progression of my character? I start from A, and I've got to get to Z. But the character seems so loaded in the beginning that I feel I'm tipping the ending from the moment I come on. What should I do?"

Meg

Dear friend,

I should be grateful to the actor for bringing up the question of his character's progression. It's what we have to work on. Obviously the play can't be tipped all at once. If Jerry is menacing right from the start, you have to wonder why Peter just sits there and takes it. Why doesn't he get off the bench and go somewhere else? Jerry has to seduce Peter at the same time that he is provoking him. What I mean by *seduce* is to be charming, witty, unusual, interesting.

I also have to pay attention to the actor playing Peter. A trap is that Jerry is so complex that I can forget to direct Peter.

What does each character want?

Peter wants:

A quiet afternoon away from it all.

An escape from his family life.

To enjoy his book.

After Jerry enters Peter wants:

To pay him as little mind as possible.

To be polite so that he'll go away.

To try to figure him out.

To protect his bench.

To fight for what is his.

To stop this craziness.

To get back control.

Peter's objective in the play changes. He goes from wanting to have a pleasant day to fighting against abuse.

Jerry wants:

To be interesting.

An audience.

To share his life with another person.

To understand his own life.

Another person to understand his life for him.

To find something meaningful.

A fight.

To provoke Peter out of his complacency.

Peter to put the knife in him.

Meg

Dear friend,

Rehearsals are going better. The more charming and off-handed Jerry is, with only a slight edge of aggression, the more he compels Peter to take an interest in him.

Peter's part is much more difficult because it's not as showy and because he has to do an amazing amount of concentration to listen to Jerry. The audience will focus on his moment-to-moment reactions and respond accordingly. If he's shocked or annoyed, I know that the audience members will laugh. If he's at all frightened, they will be, too.

The last hour of rehearsal yesterday I asked the actors to put down their scripts and improvise the whole play. I wanted them to forget the words of the text and, like jazz musicians, take whatever was happening between them wherever it went. At first they just clung to the text. I stopped and told them to find their own words and their own responses. That helped for awhile, but I found that they were doing a lot of playwriting: That is, they talked endlessly about things we didn't have to know. I stopped them and suggested that they use words sparingly and say only what they wanted to, nothing more. The improv took off. They were both very free and spontaneous. But they ran out of steam around the time they fought over the bench. They were fatigued from doing the kind of concentrated work they're unused to. But if I can sustain that "real life" impromptu feel they had in the improv when they're acting the text, my goals for this show will be achieved.

We had an interesting discussion after rehearsal. It concerned Jerry's act of killing himself. I have to confess that, although I understand it intellectually, I don't really relate to it. The actors had various ideas but were looking to me to give a satisfying explanation. I couldn't and felt that by the time we left they thought that because I'm a woman, I wouldn't understand Jerry's intention. I'm beginning to feel that as the director I'm overlooking something very important. (Hoping lightning strikes soon.)

Meg

Dear friend,

Why does Jerry want to kill himself?

Where was Jerry before he entered, and what was he doing?

I tried answering these questions by improvising with the actor playing Jerry. He began to feed the pigeons in the park, and I asked him, "Talk out loud and express what you think is buzzing inside Jerry's head."

He walked around the room and picked up various objects and said,

I want to be here.

I want to feel good.

I want to feel better than I do.

I want something.

I want someone.

I want a lover.

I want a dog.

I want a friend.

I want a life.

I want to kill something.

Anything.

I want a knife.

I want to cut these feelings out.

I want to end it all.

I want nothing.

I want nothing.

I want to forget.

I want everything to go away.

I want peace!

At one point I asked him, "Where does it hurt?" He said, pointing to his stomach, "In here. Everything is so empty." He was crying. Later he said that when he was doing the exercise he was reminded of a personal kind of loneliness he used to have. He said it was a despair that made him sick with a grief he didn't understand. He said it made him angry as well. It made him furious to be a "have-not" when everyone around him had so much more.

We began rehearsals, and I must say that he was possessed with a genuine pain and yet at the same time with a humor that covered it. He was coming very close to the character.

It dawned on me that we had to play his compulsion to die one of two ways. The first is that he had been to the zoo and seen the kind of disconnection between the animals and people watching them, which reminded him of his relationship with the dog he tried to kill. Jerry is also disconnected from his own self. His life is like watching someone else's home movie. He has a vision of his own death. He wants to die and enters, sees Peter, and uses him to attain that goal.

The second way of playing it is to enter, full of self-loathing and guilt over what he did to the dog, see Peter, start talking just to talk, and finally confess to this stranger what he's done to the dog. The suicide is not premeditated. It just happens impulsively. In other words, he's behaving on a very intuitive and subconscious level.

We tried the first way, and it seemed contrived to me. The play took on a very direct course. Jerry was so interested in the ending that he couldn't care less about what was happening between him and Peter until then.

The second way—the spontaneous and irrational way—worked better for me. For one thing, after Jerry confesses his horror story, and all Peter can say is, "I don't understand," an enormous recognition happened for Jerry. He realized that he is not understood. He has spilled his guts and can get nothing but incomprehension in return, which enrages him. He hit Peter out of contempt for his obtuseness and stupidity. He hit Peter because he had no other way to connect with him.

The turning point of the play came when he laid the knife at Peter's feet and got him to pick it up. That moment was very alive. Jerry crossed some line of recklessness and abandon. He made up his mind then and there! Which was far better than coming onstage with an agenda for such a dramatic action.

We all seemed to feel that we were on the right track. Watching the play moved me because I suddenly became a witness to events in my own life where I had experienced both Jerry's and Peter's dilemma. Funny. I didn't go into the play relating to it more than intellectually, but I'm relieved to be moved and touched by it and amazed by how it reverberates in me.

Meg

Postscript
I'll call this "lessons learned":
How closely did I stick to my "Big List"?

- My concept of complete naturalistic reality came pretty close.
- The story was always clear, except the parts that Albee leaves deliberately vague: What happened, if anything, at the zoo? The play's center is very clearly (at least to me) about the difficulty that we have connecting to each other. Or more specifically, it's about how deeply alienated so many people are, and ultimately that alienation can trigger acts of violence.
- I didn't cast the best actors I could find. I cast the actors who were available to me, but I am glad for the challenge. I'd never have cast them given other options, but they worked well and served the play. Sometimes I was too specific in rehearsals and had to learn to hold back and let the actors find things for themselves. Probably the best thing I said during rehearsals was when they were trying to execute all the actions and objectives I had sketched out: "Okay, now just forget everything I've ever said. Play it from your own responses." I was surprised by how much of the playing structure was in their bones, and yet given the chance not to act self-consciously in the pattern I'd set down, they had the pattern but made it their own.

The biggest thing I learned directing the play was when I had to decide which choice was more effective — Jerry entering with the idea of his death or that idea springing impetuously as a result of what was happening onstage. For me the lesson is that it's always more dynamic and theatrical if events like that are precipitated onstage as a result of the action. (Meaning: Characters don't psychoanalyze their every motive and action; actors and directors do. And the hard part is to keep the character knowing far less than the actor does because the character hasn't read the end of the play the way the actor has. We don't go around with scripted lives. At least I don't.)

Meg

TED'S PRIVATE NOTEBOOK

Monday. I'm beginning this journal, notebook, true confession, whatever you want to call it as a means of communicating with myself because no one around here understands me. These people are so deadly serious! I recently decided that I'd like to try the first act of *A Doll's House* as a musical, and everyone howled with laughter. The teacher turned ashen. She worships at Ibsen's shrine and thought such a "notion sacrilegious." I said it wasn't a notion, it was a concept. She said, "Prove it." She defines *notion* as an "idea-ette," a mini-spur-of-the-moment thought with no weight to it. She said a concept "was an idea that was strong enough to sustain a full evening." I told her I love musicals and think the purpose of theatre is entertainment. She obviously disapproved but said nothing. I looked around the room, and everyone was looking at the ceiling or the floor. That's because they all want to do meaningful theatre, with avant-garde sets and white lighting. I said, "My concept is to entertain the audience. Even Brecht admitted that is the principal aim of theatre!" Well, I knew when I started throwing Brecht's name around that people would begin to take me seriously. The teacher said, "But Brecht never turned Ibsen into a musical!" I admitted that but suggested that he did a whole lot worse, doing his own thing with a lot of other writers and, like Shakespeare, borrowed freely. Someone in the class said they already tried a musical of *A Doll's House*, which failed, and asked why I didn't try *Hedda Gabler* or *When We Dead Awaken*. I said that I regarded doing the first act of this play in an unconventional way as an experiment and that if I couldn't experiment at a university, where could I?

The teacher asked about my concept. I said I saw the play as a 1950s Doris Day movie set to music. The play should take place in an American city, perhaps Miami because it's Christmas, and I always find "Jingle Bells" and "White Christmas" incongruous in warm climates.

The teacher said, "It's probably very reactionary of me to ask this. But how does your concept illuminate the play?"

A fair question, I have to admit. I said, "The core of *A Doll's House* is as timely today as it was when it was written. I don't think every play has to be brought up to date in order to connect with an audience. The classics can still be done in period costume and setting and have as much validity for us today as they did when they were first presented. My problem with Ibsen . . ." At this point I didn't know if I dared go further, but I took a breath and said it: "Although he wrote all these acknowledged masterpieces, his plays are deadly dull. Like stuffed museum pieces." Because no one fainted at that remark, I went on: "Ibsen's plays are indestructible; they're built like Sherman tanks. Even if I do the most botched-up, misguided, wrong-headed production ever, the play will survive me. Won't it?"

At that point I specified:

I want the play to be funny.

I want it to be period but recent American period.

I want the play to be entertaining.

I want to take a fresh look at a play that has become the poster child of western drama.

Someone in the class asked me if I am pro- or antifeminist because that student saw the play as a great feminist tract. I said I didn't see that feminism had anything to do with the play. I believe that the play has more to do with relationships, with truth and deception and with growing up.

Tuesday. They're letting me go ahead and do the project any way I want. Probably giving me enough rope to hang myself. What I didn't tell the class and the teacher is the other reason I want to kick up the Ibsen dust: I hate the naturalistic/psychological/realism way of working that so many directors are into. If I want that, I'll go to a movie. I expect something more of the theatre!

Also, people like Meg end up becoming acting coaches. I don't think that's the director's job. The actors are there to give me what I'm after and figure out their own way how to get it. I don't have time for that stuff. I have a vision of how I want things staged, and I don't think it's too much to ask the actors to execute it with panache, skill, and expertise. This show isn't going to be about a park bench and a wacko with a knife! It's going to have style and movement—lots of movement.

I'm secretly worried that I'm being perverse. Am I doing this out of rebellion, wanting to shock my teacher, who I know doesn't approve, wanting to demolish Ibsen, working in contrary ways to the general Stanislavskian mythos around here? Yes! I'm being perverse, but it's what keeps me wanting to direct. (I wonder if other directors feel the same way.)

But the teacher is right about one thing: I should keep asking myself how this concept illuminates the material, and as divergent as my version becomes it should have some integrity about Ibsen's original intentions.

Wednesday. I'll tell you how I relate to old Henrik's intentions. I have no patience for lying and liars. I know that the play is the pursuit of the truth, and that's what I like to think theatre is all about. I think that much of life is having to please those who are above us and to suffer fools. This is why I identify with Nora. Endlessly pleasing her husband. Except she doesn't know he's a fool. She's made to feel that she's a fool whom he suffers. Even when she leaves him, what truth has she finally learned? That she's a fool who has to grow into someone wiser.

Saturday. Auditions begin. The actors are curious about why I've asked them to come in with a song. "Is this Ibsen's first musical?" one of them wanted to know. One of the girls was wonderful for Nora. Very optimistic, sunny, charming, and delightful. Perfect. She doesn't sing too well, but that doesn't frighten me as much as her reverence for the text. She holds her script like it were the Holy Bible and looks heavenward when talking about Ibsen. She said, "I hope you're doing the play straight!" I asked her what she meant. She said, "I mean this isn't going to be one of the fashionably deconstructive productions, is it?" I said, "I am going to reevaluate the play. The first act, actually, because that's all we're doing." I explained my concept, and she couldn't have been unhappier but finally said, "I love this character so much I'd play her under any circumstances." What that remark meant was that even though I seemed to be a liability to the show, she would overcome it with her optimism. A quality that I find very Nora! I'm going to use her.

The other actors seem flexible and daring, although I've told none of them where we're heading. Monday we're off and running.

Monday. First rehearsal. The actors were very prepared, having done much research on the play and the author. Nora knew her lines already, which was a pity because I had planned to cut many of them and now had to find the right moment to break the news. We read the act, and doubts began to nag at me. The play sounds much better than it reads and is extremely compelling. Was I helping it or committing an act of artistic mutilation? Terrible thoughts, best left quickly or else I'll get cold feet about the whole idea.

I blurted out my concept. "I want to do this like a 1950s sitcom." Universal silence. The girl playing Nora started to cry. I explained my rationale for the sitcom. Nora said, "So I'm supposed to be Doris Day? But Doris Day was manipulative and totally in control over every situation, especially with men. Nora's not in control at all in that department. She tries, she thinks she is, but she's no Doris Day!"

I secretly had to admit that the actress was right. Now what? There's a big fat hole in my concept. But I pressed on, saying that tomorrow we were going to improvise some stuff and that the actors should bring in certain articles of clothing from the costume shop.

Tuesday. I brought in a whole bunch of '50s songs, and we had a rock 'n' roll party. Everyone wore '50s clothes, and our Nora wore a big blond wig. We read the act, and it began to sound like *I Love Lucy*. More like *I Love Nora*, in fact. The cast was relaxed and very open. It dawned on all of us that Nora was more like Lucille Ball than Doris Day.

We kept the party atmosphere going and decided to do an improv called "Nora, honey, I'm home!"

Nora comes in with a Yellow Cab driver who is carrying a Christmas tree and tons of boxes from Sears, while a chorus is off-stage humming a bebop version of "White Christmas." It was great fun, but in my heart of hearts I didn't know if I was adding anything or turning the play into a travesty.

I must have the courage of my convictions! Why do I keep swinging back and forth on all this? I hope that my ambivalence isn't showing because the cast members will lose morale if they sense that I'm a lieutenant afraid to lead them into combat.

My way of working is this:

I break the act down into sections or units. Some call these units "French scenes." If Nora and the taxi driver enter and play a scene together, that's a unit. When the driver leaves and Nora is alone, that's a new unit. When Nora's husband enters, that's another unit. Or French scene (the derivation of which I'm not sure).

Now, within every section is a situation. A simple, playable situation, which may be complex and complicated, but it should be clearly defined so that the audience will understand what's going on. Some refer to this as "the basic situation." For example:

French scene 1.   Nora enter with taxi driver and hides the Christmas tree. She overtips him. The chorus is singing "White Christmas." The basic situation is a woman's joy and excitement about preparing Christmas for her family. It's also about her acting like a big shot in front of the driver.

French scene 2.   Nora is alone. She sneaks some macaroons, which I've changed to a big bag of M&Ms. The basic situation here is Nora's love of sweets and the fact that she has to hide her eating them from her husband, who doesn't approve. Of course, Nora enjoys it all the more because it's forbidden.

I realized working these two small sections that Nora loves to hide things: Christmas tree, presents, candy. (Mainly what she hides is the truth!)

French scene 3.   Torvald enters. He's supposed to be working in his study, but I figured he was practicing his golf strokes and enters with a golf club. It's very suburban. When Torvald comes in I asked Nora to run over to the radio, turn it on, and dance with her husband because she's so happy. We put on some Elvis, which was fun and which Torvald doesn't like at all. She can't get him to dance, which helped their opening dialogue: You can see that she is always trying

to be upbeat and cheerful and to live for the moment, and he's uptight
and needs to control her excesses, even though he secretly is charmed
by her childishness.

We all discovered the same thing at the same time. The basic situation in this section is about their disagreement over the uses of
money. I thought that it would be great to sing "On Broadway,"
which is the ultimate fantasy about making it. Nora thinks that Torvald's job is going to get her all that money can buy, and his practi-
cality is almost ruining her dream. Nora said she was sure she could
sing the song, but the other cast members wanted to do it. What is
evolving is a chorus, commenting on the action with pop songs, while
the actors do the scenes.

I haven't decided how and where to stage the chorus. I think I'll
put it to one side of the stage.

Three days later. Last night we reviewed what we had done. It
wasn't bad, and I was very encouraging to the cast. However, Nora
thought she was being general and unspecific. I wanted to say, "Being
specific is your job! You're the actor!" But at the same time I felt
guilty that I wasn't helping her. She finds the chorus and use of music
distracting. That's it! She is subverting my concept for her narcissis-
tic need to play this classic role like a museum piece. I really should
confront her about this. I feel completely undermined by her. All that
negative energy of hers is wearing me down!

I'm being ridiculous. She's a perfectly lovely person and a talented actress. Maybe I'm throwing her too many curves. Maybe
she has to find her way, and my concept is fighting her more than
it's helping her. I must help her and try keeping my ego out of it.
This is supposed to be a collaboration, not a contest. My room-
mates tell me that I'm very high-handed with actors, and that's not
good.

Next day. My Nora seems to need a lot of T.L.C., and I have to
learn to be more supportive of the actor's process and not just my
own. We have reached a truce. She will execute what I want, but
when she asks me for reasons, I will give them, without making her
feel like she's the village idiot. (I mustn't become Torvald to her
Nora.)

Beginning of the second week. We're still working on the first three French scenes, and I haven't gotten to the rest of the cast yet.

Questions I keep asking myself:

Is this concept working?

Wouldn't things be better if I cut a lot of the dialogue because the music and movement say it all?

Are the other actors who I haven't gotten to getting upset?

Shouldn't I barrel on ahead, sketch everyone's role out, then go back and work more specifically?

Why do we get only three and half weeks to do this kind of work?

Did I bite off more than I can chew?

Middle of the second week. We're working on the scene between Nora and Mrs. Linde. Talk, talk, talk for days! Of course, it's important because it portrays a number of revelations, such as Nora's loan from Krogstad and her pride at having been so resourceful. It also contains a major turning point for Nora, one that she is not aware of: that helping Mrs. Linde get a job in her husband's bank threatens Krogstadt enough to blackmail Nora. The girls playing the scene said it reminded them of Vivian Vance and Lucille Ball on *I Love Lucy* because Lucy is always going around Ricky's back and getting herself into hot water. The question was how to set the scene. I tried moving the scene into Nora's bedroom where the ladies were trying on lots of clothes. That didn't work.

Tried doing it to shape-up exercises, which wore the girls down, and they had no breath to play the scene.

Then I had a brainstorm. I thought: Why not just sit down and play the scene with a pot of coffee and loads of cookies? Although it's not active physically, there's a lot of storyline and plot to hold interest.

The actresses were delighted. One of them pointedly said under her breath, "Of course, this is what I've been saying all along. Why don't we just sit and play the scene?"

I said, "Why don't you do it like Lucy and Ethel?" They did, and it was hilarious. Even Nora, our keeper of the flame Ibsen, had fun playing it that way.

The teacher asked me how things are going. I confessed that I was confused. I didn't know if what I was doing was merely perverse, a gimmick, or had any value whatsoever! I also told her I was worried that I hadn't gotten to several of the actors in the play yet.

She seemed to appreciate my honesty and left saying, "George Abbott, the famous Broadway director, used to stage his show in three days. He'd do an act a day and on the fourth day have a run-through. After he saw the play on its feet, he began to break it down in detail. You are doing only an act and have spent ten days on less than half of it. I think you should get it pulled together very quickly now and give all your actors a sense of where they are going."

Good advice.

Next day. I roughed out the rest of the act. Then did a run-through. This is what I see:

A concept that may or may not be working. It looks like we're in the 1960s and somewhere in Florida or L. A., having a very warm Christmas. The Elvis songs in the background are fun but sometimes interfere with the dialogue onstage. The actors who sing offstage really should be brought on, maybe to one side of the stage as a modern Greek chorus. But to tell the honest truth, what I have seems to fall between two stools. It's neither Ibsen nor a departure. I know I should be taking my concept as far as it can go, but somehow I find myself holding back. I should use less dialogue and have the actors speak in their own words and call the piece "Variations on a Theme by Ibsen."

But, of course, the actors have learned their lines and love them. If I separate them from what they know, they may become panicked.

But the bottom line, the fundamental question nags at me: Is this concept adding anything to the play, or is it just a gimmick?

Also. Am I doing all this because I think the play is so great that it can handle, like Shakespeare, any representation, or am I trying my best to destroy it? Or in my great quest to end psychological naturalism onstage am I creating a wish on the audience's part to bring it back?

I must press on. Right or wrong, I must go for the concept I've started. I'm in the thick of it now, and there's no way out. First thing tomorrow, I'm going to cut a lot of lines. We don't need them.

Two days left before the performance. The actors are totally confused. They don't know which lines are in and which have been cut.
No one seems to have a through line. In short, nothing works. Everything seems to be in the way of everything else: the improvised lines
with the written lines, the movement with the intentions of the characters, the music with the basic situation of each scene. I can't believe
the chaos I've wrought. Somewhere the play has been lost. I have
"Variations on Nothing."

The performance. The actors were wonderful. They pulled it all
together, and the audience found the piece screamingly funny. I sat
there stunned. Afterward, I bumped into the teacher, who said,
"You've turned Ibsen into the best sketch writer *Saturday Night Live*
has ever had. You must be very proud of yourself!" Which I interpret
as meaning: "You reduced a treasure of world dramatic literature to
pop fodder with your revisionist mishandling."

Conclusions

- Maybe the teacher is right. Maybe I've reduced rather
  than heightened or illuminated Ibsen's intentions with my
  concept.
- Maybe just because the audience is laughing at something, it's
  not necessarily the right kind of laughs. Maybe the audience
  laughed at the dumbness of things rather than at insights into
  the absurd nature of human behavior.
- I know that I must do more preparation on my concept the
  next time. I spent too much time rehearsing every idea that
  popped into my head and no time rehearsing the actors. If I
  want to work in such an impromptu fashion I need much
  more time.
- Did I achieve my twin goals of entertainment and nonnatural-
  istic acting? In a way I did.
- But did I gut a masterpiece to do so? By violating so much
  of the text, I did. Is that a terrible thing? Does that show
  that I have no integrity for the work of authors, only self-
  interest in my own ideas? I don't know. I have to think a lot
  about that.

- I want to reinvent theatrical experience, not reproduce it the same way that it's been done for hundreds of years.

Brainstorm: I'm thinking of doing *Hamlet* on a gurney, under operating lights, and with most of the characters in his life played by puppets. We find out later that it all takes place in an insane asylum. I think it's a strong concept and will propose it for my next production.

PART FIVE

A SYMPOSIUM WITH YOUNG DIRECTORS: ON QUESTIONS ABOUT DIRECTING

CHAPTER TWELVE

A SYMPOSIUM

The following extracts are from an ad hoc symposium attended by a few directors who had recently finished an undergraduate theatre program, a number of directors currently enrolled in an MFA directing program either in theatre or film, and several who had completed programs and were working professionally. What I wanted to know from them were the questions that they found themselves asking, questions that neither books nor their teachers had answered. Admittedly, there are questions that only life, work, and experience can answer. Nevertheless, I wanted to know what is on the minds of young people who are trying to build a craft and technique for themselves as directors. (For the sake of simplicity, I've synthesized the group into three voices and myself.)

LEADERSHIP

Director 1: The one thing that I've found lacking in books on directing or in class is how to be an effective leader. It's important to spearhead a production and be able to focus on whatever concept, idea, or story you're working on. But you have to deal with so many people, so many different egos. How do you form a collective team?

Director 2: I keep reminding myself that just because I'm the director doesn't mean I have all the answers.

Mel: When you don't have all the answers, do you admit it?

Director 2: Yes, absolutely. I think the team accepts that and respects it. And if someone has a better idea than my own, it leaves me free to consider it, use it, and benefit from it.

Mel: Are we saying that leadership has more to do with sharing than it does with dictating?

Director 2: In my case it does. I don't want to be a dictator. But I want what I want.

Mel: That's the key. You can be sharing, loving, helpful, open, have the patience of a saint, be flexible to the ideas of others, but the constancy of your own beliefs can only help inspire those around you. I once heard an actress who worked with Brecht for years at the Berliner Ensemble. She said, "We spent hours discussing, sharing ideas, giving our various points of view, and in the end, did exactly what Mr. Brecht wanted us to do."

Leadership has a lot to do with respect. It's not about how your company respects you as much as how you respect it. I've seen directors be very negative with their actors, treat them like untalented fools. I've heard people around a production say of their director, "She's so uptight, just look at the tension in her body, like she's about to have a fistfight." Or there's the director who is indiscreet and talks about an actor or a designer behind his back. If you don't respect the people you are working with, the feeling will be mutual. You can certainly feel differently about people and certainly be aware that some may be at a different level of skills. Those at a lower level need your attention more. Respect means you can't demean anyone's talent. After all, what are you leading anyway? A group of gifted people who are doing their best to serve the play and your vision of it.

Director 1: Another aspect of leadership is knowing how to organize.

Director 3: Like rehearsal schedules? I find I'm still confused about how they should be organized, what to rehearse when, for how long, when to tell the actor what—that sort of thing.

SCHEDULING

Mel: Consider the actors who have to perform the play. They have to learn the text, learn your staging, and eventually make both organic. They have to find their characterizations as well as all the nuances and colors of the text. They have to go from working in a rehearsal room to a theatre, from wearing street clothes to putting on makeup and costumes, from working under fluorescent lights to stage lights, from playing to you and the stage manager to hundreds of people.

Consider the designers who have only the tech and dress rehearsals to pull all their work into a final phase.

In other words, rehearsals are not only for the director to try out his or her ideas. They're for everyone involved in the production. Part of the psychology of scheduling is for the director to give all concerned the opportunity to do their work.

What conditions the schedule is the factor of time. How long is the play and how much time do you have to rehearse? If you have a long play and a short amount of rehearsal time, the work is liable to be unspecific and general.

Directors have to cultivate an inner sense of timing that tells them when to get the show ready. Push too fast, and your show will work wonderfully in rehearsals but be stale by opening. Obsess over the same scenes time and again, and the show will never be ready.

Director 1: Is there a specific week-by-week method?

Mel: Yes and no. Think of things this way instead:

1. You want to give the actors a sense of the progression of the play and their roles as soon as possible, not from reading, but from having experienced the play on its feet. Some directors have run-throughs very soon. But all that some directors do is run through the play over and over, like a drill. This can lead to

diminishing returns because all you're doing is compounding what doesn't work into playing habits. I usually err on the other side, which means I don't have run-throughs until very late in rehearsal. I get so intent on the specifics of every moment that I leave myself and my actors almost no time to see what we've really got until the tech rehearsal is upon us.

It's better to see some rough sketches of the play, without all the specifics you want, just to get a feel of where you are and where you have to go.

2. You don't want actors to hang around the greenroom all day and not use them. It makes them nervous and insecure and creates a lot of negative energy around a production. They feel that they are not getting the work they need. Also, if you've made a call, try adhering to it. If you're working on a two-person scene at ten but have called the entire cast for eleven and don't get to the cast members until four, you've sapped from them the energy they initially came to work with.

3. Try not letting whole acts of the play languish. That is, if you've staged the first act and find yourself spending weeks on the second act, the next time you come back to act 1 the work will have vanished. Always keep everything you've done alive by getting back to it periodically. Even if you have to tell the actors, "I just want to review the act, sketchy as it is. We'll make it specific and find the details later on."

4. Add something to rehearsals each day: new adjustments, new insights, a piece of business that enlivens the action, an adjustment to the playing that the actors would like to try. Unless it's special choreography or a fight scene that demands precision and accuracy, you want to find fresh impulses and make new discoveries.

5. If you are running through the play, leave time in the next day's rehearsal to work your notes. You can't always fix what doesn't work by a discussion. You need time to guide the actors through new adjustments by restaging them.

MIND GAMES

Director 1: I often feel that I'm playing mind games with my actors, and I hate that.

Mel: What do you mean?

Director 1: Often I don't say what I really believe. If something is lousy, I don't come right out and tell the actor.

Director 2: Telling an actor that he's lousy isn't the most creative move you can make.

Director 1: I know that, and I don't. But as a result, I find that I compromise in the wrong way. I settle for something I don't really want.

Mel: It seems that it's the actor who's playing the mind games on you and winning.

Director 3: I think it's a question of pushing the right buttons in the actor.

Mel: Explain.

Director 3: Directors are expected to be encouraging and nurturing.

Mel: Back to leadership, yes.

Director 3: We have to figure out how we're going to get through to the actor and have him achieve what we want.

Director 2: Sometimes it's an issue of semantics. You have to be able to say just the right thing that hits the actor.

Director 1: But that's the manipulation—the mind game. All this conjuring of things to put inside the actor's head.

Mel: Actors play mind games on themselves by pretending to be other people. They manipulate their own experiences into those of their characters. Do you truly believe they mind your manipulation of them? They expect it. They are waiting to make the connections between what you want and what they have to play. You just keep talking, working, trying until you hear the "click."

Director 2: Isn't it a good idea to spend time with your cast after rehearsals, going out, having drinks, and so forth?

Director 3: I don't think so. They need time alone, away from the director, to complain, ventilate, be free from our control.

STORYTELLING

Director 1: I think it's my job to tell the story. But I'm often concerned with what part of the story the audience is getting.

Director 2: I think they should be entertained along the way.

Director 1: Entertained, but isn't there more to it than that?

Director 3: I think we have to educate the audience.

Director 1: I hate didactic theatre. If I want to be educated, I'll open a book. I don't need to be preached to in the theatre.

Director 3: An audience comes to the theatre to learn, to experience, to be enlightened.

Director 2: To have a good time!

Mel: Maybe everything you're suggesting is possible. But let's get back to storytelling.

At a given point in rehearsal, usually towards the dress rehearsal, or certainly by the previews, the director has to ask, "What is the audience getting out of this show?" Meaning not so much to what degree it's being entertained, as how effective is the story that is being told.

Director 2: Are there general principles about this?

Mel: There used to be. For example, you would hear a producer or a critic say, "I don't like this play, because I don't like the central character." So everyone would scramble to make the central character likable. The hero or heroine had to be characters you empathized with, felt compassion towards, and rooted for.

Director 3: That's certainly not the case today. I love Orton and Mamet's plays and hate everyone of their characters.

Mel: Exactly. They're a bunch of rogues living by their wits, but that's the point of the plays. In the not too distant past, one person, however, would have to be what is called "redeemable."

Director 2: Redemption is for coupon savers.

Mel: It was also imposing morality of a certain kind on drama. Sinners had to be redeemed. For me, however, I don't believe a character has to be likable or savable; he or she has to be understandable. And I believe that is what theatre today gives us: a gallery of characters, many of whom are enigmatic, problemed and lost, but understandable.

I want to be able to comprehend characters. And by that I don't need a whole lot of analytic background on them. In some cases, I don't even have to know why characters are doing what they're doing. It doesn't have to be laid out clinically for me. If I understand on the most subliminal level what informs the characters behavior and action, I am compelled by them and want to figure out the rest myself.

Director 2: Along with this, wasn't there, or I should say, isn't there the idea that characters should grow and change in the course of the play for the audience to have a satisfying experience?

Mel: Yes, this growth had to have happened to the protagonist. And this is where the learning experience happened—for both the audience and the characters.

Director 3: This brings us back to recognition, and the recognition of the truth.

Mel: But it's fully possible that the characters in a play have learned nothing, that they in fact have grown backwards.

Director 3: Growth backwards is still a growth, so maybe it's dramatically viable.

Mel: That's right. Look at the characters in Mamet's *Sexual Perversity in Chicago*. The one character who moved ahead ends up as backward as the guy who never moved.

Director 1: Or if there is neither movement forward or movement backward, there can be stasis.

Mel: Yes, and staying motionless after all attempts to move and grow can be dramatic.

Director 2: Like Beckett. "We must go on, we will go on," and they stay in place.

Mel: So these so-called principles around storytelling such as likable characters, the characters learning something, etc., are not real principles. They become exigencies of the marketplace. Formula movies and television are made from them. They comfort the audience and give the impression this is what life should be about. But they do help you reflect on these questions:

1. What is the audience getting out of the story?
2. The central characters are very unlikable, but are they understandable?
3. Is the point of the play being made, even though its story is not all that safe and comfortable for the audience?
4. Have I missed any turning points, especially at the end of the story, which give either the character or the audience insight into the situation?
5. Do we feel the hero or heroine has learned and grown in any way? If not, is it the point of the play or a failure of direction?

COMEDY

Director 3: How do you cast for comedy?

Mel: It depends on the type and style of the comedy and how you intend to direct it. It also depends on who you are, where you are, where you've been in your life, and your view of the world. This doesn't mean that you have to be a person who is happy and gay. You can be quite the opposite, but it helps if you see the human condition as absurd and somewhat ridiculous.

If you are casting a comedy that is particularly physical you need actors who are skillful in that area. Comedy that is verbal, with special language requirements, demands another kind of expertise. Then there is the comedy that demands both.

When you are reading the actor make sure that he or she can handle either the verbal or the physical needs of the text. The verbal is easy. Your ears will be immediately struck by how the language tumbles out of the actor's mouth. Are the jokes there, does he make you laugh, is his personality suited to the spirit of the role? Is he too cartoony, is he too heavy handed, is he too remote, is he vulnerable enough, is he too vulnerable, is he passionate enough to pursue the character's intentions, is his vocal potential varied enough, or is he going to be on one note throughout? Ascertaining physical plasticity and expert use of his body is another matter. Here you may want to improvise with the actor. If you have a lot of pratfalls in mind and find out that the actor has had recent injuries, you have to know that you'll either cut the pratfalls or get another actor.

Does the actor find the material funny? I've had actors come in and tell me they don't know why the script is called a comedy. If they don't have a sense of humor about the material, it's not usually a good idea to pursue them any further.

Director 3: I tend to cast funny-looking people in comedy. I like very oddball types and actors who are physically different than each other. I like a goofy look to what I'm doing.

Mel: Well, okay. But I've seen perfectly good-looking actors play against their type and be good and goofy, too.

Director 2: Jokes bother me. How do you do the joke, get the laugh, but not look like you're doing a sitcom?

Mel: Jokes aren't necessarily cheap little devices to keep the audience awake. Molière, Chekhov, Shaw, O'Neill, even Arthur Miller and Tennessee Williams, not to mention Shakespeare and Euripides, used them. You get the laugh when the jokes come out of the situation and spring from the behavior of the character. You don't necessarily have to face the audience and dump the comedy into its lap. But the director has to know the following:

1. Where the jokes are in the script.
2. How to stage them.

As for where they are, there are times when you think that something is a joke, and it's not funny to the audience. At other times the audience will laugh at things you never dreamed were funny. An Alan Ayckbourn play will read like there are no laughs at all: That's how integrated the jokes are with the characters and the situation.

As for staging jokes, there are many theories, rules, and axioms, such as, "No one on the stage should move while the person with the laugh line says it." This is perfectly ridiculous. If there are many laugh lines, it would mean everyone onstage would be frozen most of the time. The idea is to have continuity of action and activity so that the joke springs surprisingly and naturally from its source.

Along with the notion of having everyone freeze during the laugh line was the notion that the joke had to be pointed downstage as though it was being delivered to the audience. I've heard wonderful laughs with the actor almost upstaged on the line. If the staging seems "true," in character, and if the dramatic tension of the scene is strong enough, you should be able to get the laugh. If anything, you don't have to be in the audience's face on every joke. You just have to arrange the staging in such a way that the focus is on the actor with the joke.

Often the laugh will come not from the line, but rather from the other character who has to react to the line. That's the moment that you want in the audience's lap. That's the moment that you don't want upstaged. A joke is like a stick of dynamite that the character ignites as he says it and tosses it onto the character receiving it for the explosion. Comics love to "walk out of the laugh." That is, they say the joke and walk away as though nothing happened. It stuns the audience and the listener. You'll notice in sitcoms and movies today that the person who has the joke is cut away from almost instantly in order to get the take from the listener. Also, the director has to keep "the egg off his actors' faces." There may be a big joke that you've set up but no laugh. If the actor who said the joke has no behavior or activity after saying it, he's just going to be standing there in embarrassed silence hoping that another actor comes in on cue immediately. That's why you need to keep the flow going all the time in comedy. Say the joke and move on to your next action.

Director 1: It seems that there needs to be more truth in comedy than in a serious play. What I mean by *truth* is a certain kind of believability for the audience no matter what the style is. I once saw a *commedia dell'arte* piece and found myself completely immersed in the world of masks, acrobatics, and lunacy as much as I'd been watching Eugene O'Neill.

Director 2: What are some of the pitfalls in directing comedy?

Mel: Being fake, artificial, forced, pandering for laughs— bad acting, in other words. But more importantly, be aware that it's very easy to be excessive and go overboard on schtick and invention. Comedy for me is very addictive, and I don't always practice what I preach. I'm telling you to find the truth, not be obvious, not to do funny business for the sake of itself, not to get hooked on the audience laughing to the point that you try for more and more and more. But I have succumbed to those temptations. I've taken a laugh that was ten seconds long and worked it into a two-minute routine. And the audience went with it, loved it, but in effect was leading me up a blind alley because I lost the play and the context for the comedy. I bent the play out of shape. Now what I try to do, seductive as the laughs are, is to stick to the story, the situation, and the characters and find not only what is funny, but also what is true. And I sometimes sacrifice a laugh or two if it hurts the story or situation.

There are good laughs and bad laughs. The good laughs spring from the situation. The bad laughs are imposed, decorative directorial devices that have nothing to do with the story but point attention to their perpetrator.

If you study the films of Charlie Chaplin, Buster Keaton, Laurel and Hardy, the Marx Brothers, and so forth, you will find routines in the middle of each story that are brilliantly inventive. They are filled with extraordinary set pieces of "stage business" that come from the situation and use of props or objects. Ladders, revolving doors, pies, automobiles, beds, dishes, animals, cement, bricks, feather pillows, the list is endless. These characters are always getting into trouble or causing trouble by these routines. The spirit of their comedy is anarchy. When you watch a hundred people throwing pies at each other, you know that the world has gone berserk and is perilously out of control.

The pitfall onstage is to create routines that don't come from the characters' intentions but that instead come from an arbitrary desire to make the audience laugh. All these film comedians played the little guy who's trying to make it, trying to get it right. Even Molière's *Misanthrope*, who is hardly a little guy, is trying to get it right, and we laugh at him because he's going about it all wrong.

Director 3:   Isn't pacing very important in comedy?

Mel: Pacing is important in any play, but the misconception is that faster is funnier. It's not. Comedy has to have an effortless, unforced rhythm and needs to breathe. There has to be dramatic tension, real need on the part of the characters and a variety of unexpected dynamics. I've seen many comedies revved up to manic heights, played at breakneck speed as though everyone on the stage had a train to catch. It's the kind of jabbing and hammering at audiences that they don't appreciate.

Director 3:   What about timing?

Mel: Timing means how the actor is picking up the cue and the rate at which he says the line. All this has a great deal to do with the performer's and director's instincts. The whole idea of timing is academic until the audience comes in. At that time, it's pretty much in the actor's hands, or I should say, in her ears as to how she's listening both to the other actors and to the house. The actor has to sense just the right moment to come in with her line. If she over-times the moment, meaning she's waited too long, she may lose the laugh. If she comes in too soon, she may not give the audience a chance to hear the cue. Needless to say, the director's presence during the previews of a comedy is when a good deal of the work on timing is done.

Timing means entrances and exits and who comes in when. The director has to work out exactly when the actor leaves the room and another comes in. Cues can't be fully realized until you're working on the set, but the idea is to make these as clean and seamless as possible. I suggest that you work by the numbers in certain routines, especially those dealing with doors and complex stage business. This means counting out the timing musically. "Exit, count three, and return. Look around and count three and exit. Slam the door, count four, and reenter through the other door," and so forth.

Timing means when stage business is executed. If someone just got a big laugh on a joke, and another actor has a hilarious piece of business coming up with a prop, he's obviously going to ride the laugh of the joke before he begins his business. Otherwise, he kills the laugh on the joke by cutting into it and lessens the impact of his physical gag.

Timing means knowing when to bring the lights up and when to bring them down. Do you want a blackout, or is a blackout too abrupt? Do you want a fadeout in five seconds or ten? Many directors don't know when to get offstage, which means that they allow moments that they are in love with lingering endlessly. It is like watching a film where there is no cutting from scene to scene. There are only slow dissolves.

Director 3: How do you know when something's funny?

Mel: When I laugh.

Director 3: Do you laugh all the time, like some directors do to encourage their actors?

Mel: Do you?

Director 3: I try to, yes.

Mel: So do I. I can watch something hundreds of times and think it's funny. The danger is that when you stop laughing the actors become very alarmed: "You didn't laugh today; is something wrong?"

Director 3: I just worked with a director who led the audience in the laughs. He laughed a beat before the joke was done in order to signal that everyone should laugh. It drove the actors on stage nuts.

Director 2: When the actors or the crew laughs, is it a good sign?

Mel: It's a sign that you will never get the same laugh from an audience. Those are laughs from insiders and have nothing to do with how the public will receive the show.

Director 1: Does music help comedy?

Mel: Some directors use preshow music to jolly up the house. Others use underscoring and music between the scenes. Music is a powerful tool that sets the mood and tone of the play. I once did a comedy, and the audience came into the theatre in silence and stayed that way until the curtain went up. I couldn't understand why the audience was so quiet. It was like the audience entered a tomb and was waiting to be sealed up. I asked the sound technician to record an audience at intermission with all its chatter and hubbub. We did and played it before the show. It helped the actual audience members to loosen up and talk to one another. After one of the performances that went poorly, someone suggested that we go out, find a comedy that was working, and record the laughs as well.

ALSO BY MEL SHAPIRO,
AN ACTOR PERFORMS

INTRODUCTION*

This book is about how actors use the world of imagination to achieve a performance. It is about using imagination to explore the text, using imagination to open yourself as an actor, and using imagination to search for the essence of the character you're performing. This book is for beginning, intermediate, and advanced students of acting. It is also for working professionals with many years of experience. The difference between the levels is made by skill and knowledge gained from experience. But the problems on all levels are the same: understanding the text, finding a viable interpretation, dealing with the language of the play, and using one's body and mind and imagination to create a fully realized performance in the part.

This book is called *An Actor Performs* in the belief that the actor, during an exercise, a scene in class, a rehearsal for a production, and finally on stage, is always performing. The best work is the work that is "out there," being performed. Actors shouldn't be thought of as having an internal Cuisinart in their psyche that grinds down their own experiences for them to pour back into their own veins for the benefit of only themselves. Unless those experiences are performed they remain unexpressed, uncommunicated, and of what theatrical use?

---

* Read the following introduction to learn more about *An Actor Performs,* published by Harcourt Brace College Publishers (ISBN: 0-15-502919-3).

This book is divided into five parts.

Part One deals with the tools. These are a creative use of the actor's biography, techniques for reading and analyzing plays, an awareness and usage of language, and skills in making effective acting choices.

Several years ago I developed an exercise called "autodrama." I felt that many young actors thought that "acting" or "performing" is something that you apply on top of your own self or put on like a mask at Halloween, that acting is getting up there and strutting around, using fancy language, being larger than life, and generally imitating bad acting. I wanted the actor to know that he or she could be simple, honest, autobiographical, and theatrically viable without laying on a lot of effects. Autodrama has become the first exercise I do with a new class, whether it's a group of precollege students or a group of seasoned professionals. As you develop skills in using your own experiences, it is very important to understand that you must develop your reading and text analysis skills at the same time. All this goes hand in hand along parallel lines.

It's surprising how few acting classes deal with text. The assumption is that because students get a smattering of text analysis or play reading as freshmen or sophomores, they should know it! It doesn't work that way. Play analysis is usually not taught from an actor's point of view, and unless it is ongoing and integrated with acting, total amnesia on the subject occurs in the senior year. As long as acting students and teachers are content to believe that reading skills are not a part of an acting book or an acting class, we are training actors who are one hundred percent dependent on their directors and teachers for "interpreting" the text for them.

Art, like life, is about solving problems. You have to experience the solution for yourself so you can solve the problem when it comes up the next time. The irony is that while others are making both your artistic and intellectual choices for you, you are the one who's going to be on stage doing the performance. And if you really can't read a text in a way that opens it up to your own imagination and helps you own the role, what you end up giving the audience is an empty result. I hope the chapters on Reading the Text (Objectively), Language, and Reading the Text (Subjectively) will help you become a contributing member of the production team.

Part Two is about the process. Process is the slow, developmental growth of layer upon layer of autobiography, text skills, and acting technique into a way of working. The key to having a way of working that connects the tools into the process is imagination.

The exercises in this book are designed to extend the actor's imagination into the world of the play and into the private experiences of the character. The actor needs to create a bridge from himself to the character and back again. How do you relate to the character? Are your life experiences analogous? What if they are not? There is a series of improvisations and exercises that can create as much useful memory as experiences you might have lived.

Part Three explores putting together the work done on the use of tools and process into characterization, which is where all roads eventually lead. Living the life of your character through particular improvisations, exercises, and research techniques is illustrated. A system of asking yourself certain questions, asking your character certain questions, and using a diary is examined in detail.

Extending the actor's range via comedy, one-person shows, cabaret, and performance art constitutes Part Four. These areas can be viewed as advanced work. However, they can be encouraged as extracurricular activity or can be approached at the same time as other work is taking place. (There are times when I wonder if work on comedy and cabaret should not be the beginning of actor training.) These areas go to the heart of actors' empowering themselves. An idea whose time has come.

Part Five is an interview with three actors on the nature of performing on stage and on camera. The actors are Ron Leibman, who won a Tony for Best Actor playing Roy Cohn in Tony Kushner's *Angels in America;* Olympia Dukakis, who received an Academy Award for Best Supporting Actress for her work in *Moonstruck;* and Laura San Giacomo, who made her film debut in *sex, lies, and videotape.*

Most chapters end with a FAQ (frequently asked questions) session to summarize the points that have been discussed. These questions have all been asked in one class or another, time and again. Asking questions is one of the ways you learn to teach yourself.

My personal philosophy is that no one can teach you how to act. All the teacher can do is help you teach yourself because art is a slow, self-taught process that goes on for the rest of your life, or as someone once said, "Art is in the becoming."

But before we talk about art, let's talk about reading and its importance. Theatre is a branch of literature, the best of which is continually performed as the repertoire. What the audience comes to see is a story on the stage, seemingly told by actors. Actors have to know the repertoire, but more importantly they have to know how a play is built, what its structural elements are, how its story is technically being delivered, and what makes one play different from another.

It is not necessary to have read the plays cited in the exercises and examples to use this book. The extracts should be clear enough. The following plays are recommended reading. Those italicized are cited in this book.

Aeschylus	The Oresteia
	Agamemnon
	The Libation Bearers
	The Eumenides
Sophocles	*Oedipus Rex*
	Antigone
Euripides	The Bacchae
Aristophanes	Lysistrata
Kalidasa	Sakuntala
Chikamatsu	The Love Suicide at Amigima
Machiavelli	The Mandrake
Shakespeare	*Romeo and Juliet*
	Hamlet
	Twelfth Night
Racine	Phedre
Moliere	Tartuffe
Aphra Behn	The Rover
Congreve	The Way of the World
Goethe	Faust, (Parts I and II)
Ibsen	*A Doll's House*
Strindberg	Miss Julie
Wilde	*The Importance of Being Earnest*
Chekhov	*The Sea Gull*
	The Cherry Orchard

Wilder	The Skin of Our Teeth
O'Neill	*Long Day's Journey into Night*
Williams	*A Streetcar Named Desire*
	Cat on a Hot Tin Roof
	The Glass Menagerie
Hellman	The Little Foxes
Beckett	*Waiting for Godot*
	Endgame
Brecht	Mother Courage
Hansberry	A Raisin in the Sun
Genet	The Maids
Orton	What the Butler Saw
Pinter	The Homecoming
Jones	*Dutchman*
Churchill	Cloud 9
Wilson	Fences
Mamet	*Sexual Perversity in Chicago*
Shange	*for colored girls who have considered suicide/when the rainbow is enuf . . .*
Fugard	*"MASTER HAROLD" . . . and the boys*
Guare	*Bosoms and Neglect*
Kushner	Angels in America
Sondheim, Gelbart, and Shevelove	*A Funny Thing Happened on the Way to the Forum*